Flags

of the World

K. L. Jott

Flags

of the World

4880 Lower Valley Road, Atglen, Pennsylvania 19310

Translated from the German by Dr. Edward Force. This book was originally published in German by Sammüller Kreativ GmbH under the title *Flaggen Dieser Welt*.
Designed by IR
Type set in Zurich BT/ITC Officina Sans

ISBN: 978-0-7643-3635-5
Printed in China

Schiffer Books are available at special discounts for bulk purchases for sales promotions or premiums. Special editions, including personalized covers, corporate imprints, and excerpts can be created in large quantities for special needs. For more information contact the publisher:

Published by Schiffer Publishing Ltd.
4880 Lower Valley Road
Atglen, PA 19310
Phone: (610) 593-1777; Fax: (610) 593-2002
E-mail: Info@schifferbooks.com

For the largest selection of fine reference books on this and related subjects, please visit our web site at www.schifferbooks.com
We are always looking for people to write books on new and related subjects. If you have an idea for a book please contact us at the above address.

This book may be purchased from the publisher.
Include $5.00 for shipping.
Please try your bookstore first.
You may write for a free catalog.

In Europe, Schiffer books are distributed by
Bushwood Books
6 Marksbury Ave.
Kew Gardens
Surrey TW9 4JF England
Phone: 44 (0) 20 8392 8585; Fax: 44 (0) 20 8392 9876
E-mail: info@bushwoodbooks.co.uk
Website: www.bushwoodbooks.co.uk

Contents

Note: In the case of non-Latin alphabets such as Arabic, Chinese, etc., the name of the country was converted to Latin lettering.

What is a Flag?

"The word "flag" comes from English and means a symbol, made of cloth and usually rectangular, that makes known the membership in a political unit, especially a state. Today flags are so much a part of our everyday life that we often do not notice them. Whether on television, at sporting events, demonstrations, on public buildings and ships—flags are everywhere and have a message: They express membership, whether to a football team or a nation.

Flags have a long history, which we shall touch on briefly here. Then we shall portray over 200 flags with pictures and information on the history of the land and its flag. Today there are 192 sovereign states recognized by the UN. There are also several dozen lands that, now as before, fight for the recognition of their sovereignty, and others that are still crown colonies of the former ruling powers but have attained a certain degree of self-government.

The Origin of Flags

The origins of flags or their predecessors go far back. Even more than 5000 years ago, graphic symbols were used to indicate that important personalities or even gods were present at a certain place. It is known that the Egyptians used cloths on poles, similar to flags, in the 12th century before Christ to identify the various units of their troops. Through trade and war in particular, these symbols became more and more important, and they were used more frequently to make nations recognizable.

Flags in Shipping

At sea it was especially important to recognize, even at great distances and beyond shouting distance, to whom the approaching ship belonged, and whether it was friend or foe. Presumably the Vikings were the first seafarers who showed symbolic portrayals on their sails, which later were used on flags. It was also allowed in wartime to fly a neutral flag at sea to confuse the enemy. The same law, though, forbade making an attack under a false flag. Thus in a serious case the false flag had to be lowered very quickly and replaced by the right one. This practice was used particularly by pirates and freebooters who sailed the seas with the intention of capturing and plundering other ships.

Everybody probably knows the Jolly Roger, the famous black flag with the white skull and crossbones. Naturally it was only one of many pirate flags, but its gruesome simplicity made its mark.

On the high seas, flags were and are used not only for mutual identification, but also for communication with signals. At the beginning of the 18th century the first signal book appeared, from which in the following 150 years an ever-better system of

generally understood signals developed. Today there is a signals book with flags for every letter, and every number from 0 to 9. Every flag that represents a letter also has another meaning, such as "man overboard".

Today international regulations require that ships must show the flags of the countries in which they are registered. This is especially true of merchant ships and warships, but has also become very customary for private yachts.

Flags on the Battlefield

At battlefields on land too, flags played an important role, for here too they served to identify the fighting troops. In addition, great numbers of military flags were developed that made the various ranks of the soldiers recognizable. So that the flags of the various troops were also recognizable even at great distances, the tips of the flagpoles were decorated with a so-called vexilloid, often an animal figure. The Romans already used the eagle as a vexilloid.

Flags took on special meanings during the Crusades of the European Christians, beginning in the 11th century. Most of them bore a large cross on their flags, and their robes were also adorned with crosses. The colors of the crosses differed from country to country: The French and Spanish crusaders used red, the English white, the Italians blue. The idea that united all these people was the liberation of the Holy Land from the Moslems. Several modern flags go back to the crusaders' flags, for example, those of Denmark and Britain.

Flags Today

The first modern flag was that of the Netherlands. It goes back to the 16th century and was originally orange, white and blue. The simple horizontal tricolor became the forerunner of many similar flags.

Other flags are based on symbols of the patron saints of the countries. Britain's red right-angled cross is that of England's patron saint, St. George. The Scottish flag bears the diagonal white cross of St. Andrew.

Symbolism of the Colors

Colors are a particularly strong means of expression on present-day flags, and many colors have the same or at least a similar significance in many countries:

Red is often associated with blood, war and sacrifice. But it also stands for courage and revolution. The color red took on a special meaning in Soviet Russia, where it stood for revolution and socialism.

White stands for purity, innocence and peace—thus being practically the opposite of red. On many flags it also symbolizes large snowy landscapes or icebergs.

Blue often stands for righteousness, also often for peace. Sometimes it also symbolizes the sea or the sky.

Green usually represents the earth, also symbolizing the fruitfulness of a land. Beyond that, green is often the color of Islam, the favorite color of the prophet Mohammed, which naturally gives it a different meaning in most Islamic lands.

Yellow often symbolizes richness, for it is the color of gold. But yellow is also the color of the sun, which it often represents.

Black is the color of Africa and often indicates the ancestry of a people. Black also often stands for a dark past and the overcoming of enemies.

Color Combinations

The combination of red, white and blue stands for freedom. This meaning is based on the French Tricolor, on which many other flags of this world are based. The flag of the USA is also based on the same colors, which were chosen by the people, and thus it was the first flag that represented the people more than the rulers of the land. The Stars and Stripes became the model for many other flags of countries that strove for democracy. The family of the Union Jack also consists of red, white and blue. The flag of Great Britain combines the red cross on a white background of the English flag with the white diagonal cross on a blue ground of the Scottish flag and the St. Patrick's cross of Ireland. The Union Jack is in the upper left canton of the British overseas territories.

The pan-African colors of red, black, green and yellow adorn many flags of independent states in Africa. They are based on the colors of an American organization that was active at the beginning of the 20th century in sending African-born people who had been brought to America back to Africa. They were first immortalized in a flag in 1957, when the British colony of Gold Coast became the independent country of Ghana.

In many South American lands one sees variations of the Miranda flag. It takes its name from the freedom fighter Francisco de Miranda, who was one of the forerunners of the fight for freedom against the long rule by Spain and Portugal. The three equally wide stripes symbolize the separation of the New World (yellow) by the ocean (blue) from the tyranny of Spain (red).

Many Arabic lands show the same colors on their flags. This is because black and white were the colors of the Prophet and green stands for Islam. These three so-called pan-Arabic colors generally stand for the great deeds of the Moslems (white), the battles (black) and the swords (red), with green for the fields.

The pan-Slavic colors of red, blue and white are based on the flag on the Netherlands, which as noted above was the first European flag. The Russian Tsar Peter the Great was especially influenced by the clarity and simplicity of this flag and adopted the formation and colors for his merchant flag—changing only the order to white, blue and red.

Worthiness and Use of Flags

Today there is a true etiquette in the use of flags. Basically, all flags of the 192 independent countries of this world are equal—no matter whether the country is poor or rich. Consequently, flags must be set up so no country feels disadvantaged. If numerous flags are set up together, they are best arranged in a circle.

Flags must essentially be handled with respect, since they stand for a state and its Population. Many nations have established their own rules, which are not recognized internationally, for the use of their flags. Other countries, such as Great Britain, have not set up any rules of their own for the use of the Union Jack, although it is portrayed on several of the world's flags. The USA, on the other hand, has set up a catalog of rules for the treatment of national flags.

It is generally valid that flags should be hoisted only from sunrise to sunset. Sometimes the times also depend on the work times of the employees in the government buildings on which the flags are hoisted. The flags should be flown so that they fly and do not wrap around the flagstaff. The size of the flag basically depends on the event for which they are hoisted. Flags should be in good condition, not faded or torn.

One often sees flags flying at half-mast. This is done for national mourning or a state funeral. Many countries also give the flag a mourning symbol or have it bound so it cannot fly.

Flags of Organizations and in Sports

Internationally active organizations, such as the UN, NATO, EU and non-political organizations like the Red Cross also have flags to indicate their presence in a country or their internal meetings. The most famous flag in sports is surely the Olympic flag, which was designed in 1914. The white ground symbolizes peace and brotherly association. The blue ring stands for Europe, the black for Africa, the red for America, the yellow for Asia and the green for Australia.

But every soccer team has its own flag, and recently flags in stadiums have become a clear indication of a strongly felt allegiance.

Europe, because of its historical development, is regarded as an individual continent, although strictly speaking it is a subcontinent of Asia.

Europe is the second-smallest continent, with 10.5 million square kilometers. With 730 million Population, it ranks third after Asia and Africa. 75% of the population is Christian, about 8% Moslem. Europe consists of 44 independent states; the largest is Russia, the smallest the Vatican City. The largest city is Moscow, with 14.4 million Population.

Europe was influenced above all by the Greek culture, the Roman Empire and Christianity.

In the 20th century great changes took place in Europe. Through two world wars, the rise and fall of Communism, the tendency toward individual states and the counter-movement of the EU, which wants to establish an economic union. Since 1990 the number of independent states in Europe has risen from 34 to 44.

There is no natural boundary between Europe and Asia, and drawing a boundary line has often been discussed. Today it is defined by the Ural Mountains, Ural River, Caspian Sea and Sea of Azov, and for Asia Minor the Black Sea and the Bosporus. Only a quarter of Russia is in Europe, but since this quarter is the historical nucleus and 75% of the population lives there, you will find Russia in the Europe chapter.

*red dots on the maps indicate capital cities

EUROPE

EUROPE

Albania

Native name: Shqipëria (Albanian)
German: Albanien
French: Albanie
Spanish: Albania

Republic of Albania

Capital: Tirana
Area: 28,748 sq. km.
Population: 3,000,000
Languages: Albanian (official), Greek, Macedonian

Currency: Lek
Member: OSZE, UN
Economy: petroleum, metals, farm produce, textiles and shoes

A black double eagle was the family emblem of the national hero, Gjergj Skanderbeg, who led the fight for freedom from the Turks in the 15th century. This eagle, on a red ground, still adorns the Albanian flag today. According to a legend, the Albanians themselves are descended from eagles. After World War II the Communist star was placed above the eagle, but it was removed in 1992, when the flag was introduced in its present form.

Andorra

Native name: Andorra (Catalan)
German: Andorra
French: Andorre
Spanish: Andorra

Principality of Andorra

Capital: Andorra la Vella
Area: 467.76 sq. km.
Population: 66,000
Languages: Catalan (official), Spanish, French
Currency: Euro

Member: OSZE, UN
Economy: Mainly tourism; export goods are transport devices, optical and other instruments; main export country is Spain.

Andorra ranks among the world's oldest states. Its flag originally had a yellow and a red stripe, in reference to the arms of the counts of Foix and their heirs, the counts of Béarn. In 1866 Napoleon III added the blue stripe. The fields in the arms stand for the lords of the land: the bishop's mitre for the Bishop of Urgel, three bars for the Bishop of Foix, four bars for Catalonia and the cows for the counts of Béarn.

Austria

Republic of Austria

Capital: Vienna
Area: 83,871 sq. km.
Population: 8,090,000
Languages: German,
(regionally Slovenian,
Croatian, Hungarian)
Currency: Euro

Member: EU, OECD,
OSZE, UN, WEU (obser-
ver)
Economy: Main exports
are finished goods
(machines and motor
vehicles)

After World War I, Austria took up the red-white-red colors whose origins lay very far back; a legend says that the white robe of a duke was saturated with blood in combat. When he removed his sword belt, a white stripe remained to be seen. This flag was already a sea battle flag in 1786; it was introduced as the national flag only after World War I and again after World War II.

Native name: Österreich (German)
French: Autriche
Spanish: Austria

Austria and its Federal States

Burgenland
Area: 3,965 sq. km.
Population: 277,569
Capital: Eisenstadt
A golden shield with a red eagle on the red-gold colors of Burgenland.

Carinthia (Kämten)
Area: 9,535 sq. km.
Population: 559,404
Capital: Klagenfurt
Three lions, one above another, on the shield. The Hapsburgs have used these arms since 1335.

Lower Austria (Niederösterreich)
Area: 19,178 sq. km.
Population: 1,545,804
Capital: St. Pölten
Five golden eagles on a blue shield. The five-eagle arms first appeared in 1335.

EUROPE

Upper Austria (Oberösterreich)
Area: 11,980 sq. km.
Population: 1,376,797
Capital: Linz
The Austrian archducal crown, split shield with eagle. The arms date from 1390.

Salzburg
Area: 7,154 sq. km.
Population: 521,238
Capital: Salzburg
A split shield with lion and a princely crown on top. The arms originated 1284-90.

Styria (Steiermark)
Area: 16,388 sq. km.
Population: 1,183,303
Capital: Graz
A panther on the arms, with the Styrian crown over a shield. Known to exist since 1246.

Tyrol (Tirol)
Area: 12,648 sq. km.
Population: 360,168
Capital: Innsbruck
The arms show an eagle with golden arms. This form dates from 1340.

Vorarlberg
Area: 2,601 sq. km.
Population: 686,80,9
Capital: Breganz
The shield bears a red church flag and is known to exist since 1181.

Vienna (Wien)
Area: 415 sq. km.
Population: 1,631,082
Capital: Vienna
A white cross on a red shield; can also bear a black eagle.

Belarus

Republic of White Russia or Belarus
Capital: Minsk
Area: 207,595 sq. km.
Population: 9,881,000
Languages: White Russian, Russian
Currency: Belarus Rubel

Member: GUS, OSZE, UN
Economy: Exported are raw minerals, machines, vehicles, chemical and plastic products

The present flag was introduced after a referendum. When Belarus became independent in 1991, the traditional red-white-red flag was used at first. But in 1995 the flag was changed to its present form. It is reminiscent of the flag of the former White Russian Soviet Republic. The narrow band portrays a woven cloth in the pattern of the national costume. Red stands for socialism, green for agriculture and forests.

Native name: Byelarus (White Russian)
German: Weissrussland
French: Biélorussie
Spanish: Belorrusia

Belgium

Kingdom of Belgium

Capital: Brussels
Area: 32,545 sq. km.
Population: 10,376,000
Languages: Flemish, French, German
Currency: Euro
Membership: EU, NATO,

OECD, OSZE, UN, WEU Economy: Export and import concentrate strongly on the other EU countries. Most important trade goods: chemical products, metals and metal goods, machines and equipment

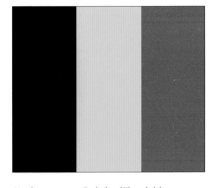

Native name: Belgie (Flemish)
German: Belgien
French: Belgique
Spanish: Bélgica

The Belgian flag is a vertical tricolor based on the French flag, but the colors come from those of the provinces of Brabant (a lion on black ground), Flanders (a lion on golden ground) and Hennegau (black and red lions on gold). The flag was introduced in 1830 when the independent kingdom of Belgium was founded, but had already flown in 1792 during rebellions against the Hapsburg overlords.

Bosnia

Bosnia and Herzegovina

Capital: Sarajevo
Area: 51,129 sq. km.
Population: 4,140,000
Languages: Bosnian, Croatian, Serbian
Currency: Convertible Mark

Member: OSZE. UN Economy: Economic life is still limited by the war. Exports are manufactured and finished goods, raw materials and machines.

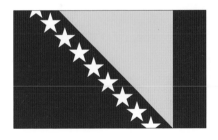

Native name: Bosna I Hercegovina
(Bosnian, Croatian)
German: Bosnien und Herzegovina
French: Bosnie-Herzégovine
Spanish: Bosnia y Herzegovina

The flag of Bosnia and Herzegovina was introduced through the UN Security Council in February 1998. The colors of dark blue and yellow and the stars are taken from the European flag. The yellow triangle symbolizes the shape of the country, as well as the three ethnic groups: Bosniaks, Serbs and Croats. The two districts of Bosniak-Croatian Federation (51%) and Serbian Republic (49%) have their own state flags.

EUROPE

Bulgaria

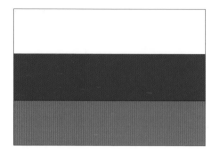

Native name: Balgarija
German: Bulgarien
French: Bulgarie
Spanish: Bulgaria

Republic of Bulgaria

Capital: Sofia
Area: 110,994 sq. km.
Population: 7,823,000
Language: Bulgarian
Currency: Leva

Member: NATO, OSZE,
UN, WEU (assoc. part-
ner)
Economy: Machines,
semi-manufactured
goods, tobacco,wine,
chemicals

In 1908 Bulgaria became an independent kingdom. In 1945 the monarchy was abolished and a people's republic proclaimed. The white stripe was temporarily adorned with a lion, the Red Star and a gear wheel. After the break with Communism in 1990 these symbols were removed. White stands for love of peace and work, green for the fruitfulness of the soil and loyalty to the homeland, and red for the bravery of the people.

Croatia

Native name: Hrvatska
German: Republik Kroatien
French: Croatie
Spanish: Croacia

Republic of Croatia

Capital: Zagreb
Area: 56,542 sq. km.
Population: 4,445,000
Language: Croatian
Currency: Kuna

Member: OSZE, UN
Economy: fuels and
lubricants, chemicals,
foods and means of
entertainment

The shield in the center of the Croatian flag has been the arms of Croatia since the 16th century. The crown on the shield consists of five different coats of arms, standing for the Croatian regions of Old Croatia, Dubrovnik, Dalmatia, Istria and Slavonia. During the Communist era the crown was replaced by a red star. But when Croatia attained independence and became a republic in 1991, the flag was introduced again in its traditional form.

Cyprus

Republic of Cyprus

Capital: Nicosia
Area: 9,251 sq. km.
Population: 770,000
Languages: Greek, Tur-
kish
Currency: Cyprus Pound

Member: EU (Greek
part), OSZE, UN
Economy: industrial and
agricultural products

The white ground of the national flag and the olive branch stand for the peaceful co-existence of the Greek and Turkish Cypriots. The island itself is shown in gold and refers to the copper deposits that gave the island its name (kypros = copper). Since the division, this flag is seen only in the Greek part of the island. In the Turkish north a version of the Turkish national flag is used. The "Turkish Republic of North Cyprus" is recognized only by Turkey.

Native name: Kypriaki Dimokratia
(Greek), Kibris Cumhuriyeti
(Turkish)
German: Zypern
French: Chypre
Spanish: Chipre

Czech Republic

Czech Republic

Capital: Prague
Area: 78,866 sq. km.
Population: 10,202,000
Language: Czech
Currency: Czech Krone

Member: EU, NATO,
OECD, OSZE, UN, WEU
(associate)
Economy: machinery,
vehicles and their parts
are exported

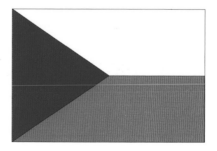

The Czech Republic, when Czechoslovakia was separated into it and Slovakia in 1993, took over the flag, while Slovakia gained a new flag. Blue, white and red are the pan-Slavic colors, and white and red are the traditional colors of Bohemia, while blue is the color of Moravia. The flag was first introduced for Czechoslovakia in 1920.

Native name: Cesko
German: Tschechien
French: République techèque
Spanish: República Checa

EUROPE

Denmark

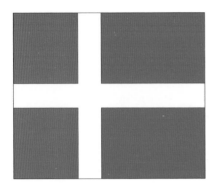

Native name: Danmark
German: Dänemark
French: Danemark
Spanish: Dinamarka

Kingdom of Denmark

Capital: Copenhagen
Area: 43,096 sq. km.
Population: 5,387,000
Language: Danish
Currency: Danish Krone

Member: EU, NATO,
OECD, UN, WEO (obser-
ver)
Economy: ship-, factory
and machinery building

The flag of Denmark is presumably the oldest national flag on earth. According to a legend, King Waldemar II saw the "Dannebrog" (Danish cloth) fall from heaven during a battle against the Estonians in 1219. Encouraged by it, the Danes won the battle. The basic pattern may be based on the red battle flag with the white cross of Christianity. Originally the cross divided the flag into four equally large parts; only later was the vertical bar moved. The external territories of the Faeroes and Greenland have their own flags.

Estonia

Native name: Eesti
German: Estland
French: Estonie
Spanish: Estonia

Republic of Estonia

Capital: Tallinn
Area: 45,227 sq. km.
Population: 1,353,000
Language: Estonian
Currency: Estonian Krone

Member: EU, NATO,
OSZE, UN, WEU (obser-
ver)
Economy: animal agricul-
ture, fishing

The Estonian flag was brought into existence by a student movement in 1881 and made the national flag in 1918, when Estonia gained independence from Russia. The blue stripe stands for the sky and loyalty, the black for the dark soil of the country and the farmers' traditional black clothing. The white stripe stands for snow and symbolizes the wish for peace and freedom.

Germany

Federal Republic of Germany

Capital: Berlin
Area: 357,030 sq. km.
Population: 82,541,000
Language: German
Currency: Euro

Member: EU, G-8, NATO,
OECD, OSZE, UN, WEU
Economy: Autos and
parts, machines, chemi-
cal products, electronics

The colors of the German tricolor are based on the uniforms of the soldiers in the times of the Wars of Liberation (black uniforms with red piping and yellow buttons). In the Middle Ages the German flag colors had been black and yellow and red and white. When the Reich was founded in 1871 the first German national flag was black, white and red. The Weimar Republic officially introduced the black-red-gold colors after World War I. Since 1949 this tricolor has been the German flag. The 16 federal states all have their own state flags.

Native name: Deutschland
English: Germany
French: Allemagne
Spanish: Alemania

Flag of the German Reich (1871-1918)
It was introduced by Bismarck in 1867. Black and white were the colors of Prussia, red the color of Brandenburg.

Federal Service Flag
Along with the national flag (above), the service flag of the German federal offices still exists. It is a symbol of the federation and may be used only by federal institutions.

Flag of the German Democratic Republic from 1949 to 1989. In 1950 the emblem of hammer, compass and circling sheaves of wheat was placed in the center. This emblem resembled that on the flag of the Soviet Union.

Baden-Württemberg

Area: 35,751 sq .km.
Population: 10,717,419
Capital: Stuttgart

The black and yellow flag of Baden-Württemberg was introduced in 1952. The colors are based on those of the states of Baden (yellow and red) and Württemberg (black and red) and the emblem of the house of Staufen, showing three black lions on a golden ground. Swabia was the home area of the ruling house of Staufen.

Bayern –
Free State of Bavaria

Area: 70,549 sq. km.
Population: 12,443,893
Capital: München
(Munich)

The colors of white (or silver) and blue were the colors of the house of Wittelsbach and of Bavaria since the beginning of the 12th century. The diamond pattern is also known since the 12th century. It comes from the heraldry of the Counts of Bogen. The Bavarian state flag exists in a form with stripes and one with diamonds.

Berlin

Area: 891 sq. km.
Population: 3,387,828

The Berlin flag shows a black bear on a white shield. The bear was first immortalized on a seal in 1280. Presumably the choice of a bear goes back to Albrecht the Bear, who founded the Mark Brandenburg in the 12th century. Above and below the white stripe are red stripes; red and white are the traditional colors of Brandenburg.

Brandenburg

Area: 29,477 sq. km.
Population: 2,567,704
Capital: Potsdam

The state colors of Brandenburg are taken from the arms of the former ruling family (Electors of Brandenburg). The eagle presumably goes back to Otto I, the son of the founder of Brandenburg. It is presumably based on the German royal eagle.

Bremen – Free Hansa
City of Bremen

Area: 404 sq. km.
Population: 663,213

The red and white flag of Bremen is based on the colors of the arms of Bremen and the colors of the Hanseatic League. Ships from Bremen took them from the colors of the empire's battle flag: a white cross on a red ground. Since 1336 the arms show the key of St. Peter, Bremen's patron saint.

Hamburg – Free Hansa
City Hamburg

Area: 755 sq. km.
Population: 1,734,830

The flag of the free Hansa city of Hamburg shows a white castle on a red ground. The castle is either the Hammaburg, built by Charlemagne in 808, or shows the fortified city with the tower of the cathedral, which is dedicated to the Virgin Mary. This castle was already shown on a seal in 1241.

Hessen

Area: 21,114 sq. km.
Population: 6,097,765
Capital: Wiesbaden

The colors of red and white are based on those of the Archbishopric of Mainz. The lion was originally the armorial animal of Thuringia, to which margravate Hesse belonged until 1247.

Mecklenburg-
Vorpommern

Area: 23,174 sq. km.
Population: 1,719,653
Capital: Schwerin

The flag is colored blue, white, yellow and red. Blue and white stand for Pomerania, blue, yellow and red are the colors of Mecklenburg. The oxhead has been on the arms of Mecklenburg since the 13th century; the griffin is the armorial animal of the dukes of Pomerania.

Niedersachsen

Area: 47,618 sq. km.
Population: 8,000,909
Capital: Hannover

The flag shows the German tricolor with a red shield on which a white horse stands. The white horse (Saxon horse of the Guelphs) comes from the arms of the dukes of Braunschweig. In 1949 it was decided to underlay the arms with the colors of the federal flag, since a combination of the traditional state colors would have made a gaudy flag.

Nordrhein-Westfalen

Area: 34,083 sq. km.
Population: 18,075,352
Capital: Düsseldorf

The flag colors, green, white and red, are based on the colors of the former Prussian province of Rhineland (green and white) and Westphalia (red and white). They are also found in the arms, which shows a shield in these colors. The left half symbolizes the Rhineland, the horse at right stands for Westphalia. The rose comes from the arms of the princes of Lippe.

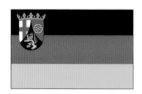

Rheinland-Pfalz

Area: 19,847 sq. km.
Population: 4,061,105
Capital: Mainz

The flag shows the German tricolor with arms at the upper left. The colors of black, red and gold derive from the arms of Rheinland-Pfalz. The arms combine those of three medieval electoral states: The red cross stands for the former Electorate of Trier, the white wheel for the Archbishopric of Mainz, and the golden lion for the Counts Palatine.

Saarland

Area: 2,568 sq. km.
Population: 1,056,417
Capital: Saarbrücken

The flag of Saarland is also black-red-gold, with its special features in the coat of arms. Each part of the arms shows the heraldic symbol of a former part of the state: the silver lion stands for Nassau-Saarbrücken, the cross for Trier, the golden lion for Pfalz-Zweibrücken and the eagle for Lorraine.

The Federal States of Germany

Sachsen –
Free State of Saxony

Area: 18,413 sq. km.
Population: 4,296,284
Capital: Dresden

White and green are the traditional colors of Saxony. The gold and black bars on the shield come from the arms of Anhalt. The wreath was originally a laurel wreath and comes from the arms of the Saxon dukes in the 13th century.

Sachsen-Anhalt

Area: 20,445 sq. km.
Population: 2,494,437
Capital: Magdeburg

The gold and black colors originated on the medieval Saxon coat of arms. In the center of the flag is a coat of arms divided in two: The upper field shows the arms of Saxony, with the Prussian eagle in the upper right corner. The lower half shows the arms of the free state of Anhalt of 1924.

Schleswig-Holstein

Area: 15,763 sq. km.
Population: 2,828,760
Capital: Kiel

The blue-white-red colors come from the state colors of blue and yellow for the duchy of Schleswig and white and red for Holstein. The two blue lions come from the Danish arms; the Holstein nettle leaf presumably from the arms of the Schauenburger.

Thüringen –
Free State of Thuringia

Area: 16,172 sq. km.
Population: 2,355,280
Capital: Erfurt

The white and red flag colors exist since 1920, when Thuringia was created out of several small states. A lion has adorned the arms of the landgraves of Thuringia since the 13th century. The eight stars on the shield represents the united lands in the founding year and the formerly Prussian areas that were added in 1945.

EUROPE

Faeroe Islands

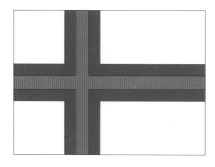

Native name: Føroyar
German: Färöer
French: Iles Féroé
Spanish: Islas Feroe

Faeroe Islands

Capital: Thórshavn
Area: 1,398.9 sq. km.
Population: 48,353
Languages: Faeroese,
Danish

Currency: Kronur
Possessor: Denmark
Economy: Main exports
are ships, fish and fish
products

The Faeroes consist of 18 islands, 17 of them populated. Since 1948 they have been an autonomous region with their own parliament and two delegates to the Danish parliament. The Population are descended from the Vikings. The islands have belonged to Denmark since the 14th century. The form of the flag and the cross are based on the Norwegian flag. A red cross outlined in blue stands on a white ground. Red and blue are traditional colors of the Faeroese; white stands for the sky and the ocean waves.

Finland

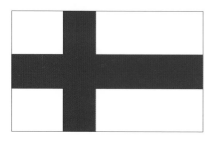

Native name: Suomi (Finnish), Finland (Swedish)
German: Finnland
French: Finlande
Spanish: Finlandia

Republic of Finland

Capital: Helsinki
Area: 338,144 sq. km.
Population: 5,212,000
Languages: Finnish, Swedish
Currency: Euro

Member: EU, OECD,
OSZE,UN, WEU (observer)
Economy: wood, optical
equipment, paper and
paper products

The white ground color of the Finnish flag symbolizes the vast snowy landscapes and the blue stands for the sky and the many lakes (over 60,000!). Before the flag was introduced in its present form in 1918, it had several variations, always based on the colors of blue and white. The form of the cross indicates Finland's being one of the Nordic states.

France

Republic of France

Capital: Paris
Area: 543,965 sq. km.
Population: 59,762,000
Language: French
Currency: Euro

Member: EU, G-8, NATO, OECD, OSZE, UN, WEU
Economy: tourism, semi-finished products, consumer goods, foods

The French tricolor has existed since 1848. Red and blue are the colors of Paris, white is the color of the house of Bourbon and is linked with both the Virgin Mary and the national heroine Joan of Arc. In addition, the colors stand for the goals of the French Revolution: liberty, equality and fraternity. The color combination was formed for the first time during the French Revolution.

Native language: France
German: Frankreich
Spanish: Francia

Gibraltar

British Crown Colony of Gibraltar

Capital: City of Gibraltar
Area: 6.5 sq. km.
Population: 27,025
Languages: English, Spanish
Currency: Gibraltar Pound

Belongs to: Great Britain
Economy: mainly tourism, also shipfitting

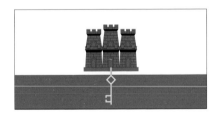

Gibraltar has the status of "British Overseas Territory." It has belonged to Britain since 1713 and was a British colony since 1830. Gibraltar has its own parliament with a governor and a head of government. The flag of Gibraltar has a wide white stripe and a narrow red one under it. On the white stripe is a castle with three towers; on the red stripe is a gold key. The castle stands for the security of Gibraltar, the key for access to the Mediterranean Sea.

Native name: Gibraltar (English)
German: Gibraltar
French: Gibraltar
Spanish: Gibraltar

EUROPE

Greece

Hellenic Republic of Greece

Capital: Athens
Area: 131,957 sq. km.
Population: 11,033,000
Language: Greek
Currency: Euro

Member: EU, NATO,
OECD, OSZE, UN, WEU
Economy: finished products, foods, machines, vehicles

Native name: Ellada
German: Griechenland
French: Grèce
Spanish: Grecia

The Greek flag symbolizes the Greek struggle for independence against the Ottoman Empire. The nine horizontal stripes stand for the nine syllables of the Greek battle cry: "Eleutheria e Thanatos" (Liberty or Death). The color blue also stands for the sea and sky, the color white for the purity of the fight for liberty. The cross stands for God's wisdom, freedom and the land. It shows Greece's link with the Orthodox church. The flag was confirmed in its present form in 1873.

Greenland

Greenland

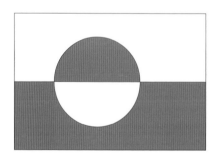

Capital: Nuuk
Area: 2,166,086 sq. km.
Population: 56,854
Languages: Kalaallisut,
Danish
Currency: Danish Krone

Belongs to: Denmark
Economy: fishing dominates; the main export is fish

Native name: Kalaallit Nunaat (Kalaallisut), Grønland (Danish)
German: Grönland
French: Groenland
Spanish: Groenlandia

Since 1943 Greenland, the world's largest island, has been an equal part of Denmark; since 1959 it has had internal autonomy. Greenland has its own parliament plus two delegates to the Danish parliament. The flag is red and white like the Danish flag. The white stripe stands for the icecap, the white semicircle for the icebergs. The red stripe represents the ocean, the red semicircle the fjords. Together the semicircles symbolize the sun.

Great Britain and Northern Ireland

United Kingdom of Great Britain and Northern Ireland

Capital: London
Area: 242,910 sq. km.
Population: 59,329,000
Language: English
Currency: Pound

Member: EU, G-8, NATO, OECD, OSZE, UN, WEU
Economy: machines and transport equipment, chemical products

In the British flag (also called the Union Jack) the symbols of the parts of the kingdom are combined: the red straight cross on white is that of England's patron saint, St. George. The white diagonal cross on a blue ground is that of Scotland's patron saint, St. Andrew. The red diagonal cross on a white ground belongs to Ireland and St. Patrick. Ireland (later only Northern Ireland) became part of the kingdom in 1801, and since then the flag has had this form.

Native name: United Kingdom
German: Vereinigtes Königreich Grossbritannien und Nordirland
French: Royaume Uni
Spanish: Reuna Unido

Hungary

Republic of Hungary

Capital: Budapest
Area: 93,030 sq. km.
Population: 10,128,000
Language: Hungarian
Currency: Forint

Member: EU, NATO, OECD, OSZE, UN, WEU (associate)
Economy: telecommunications and audio equipment, vehicles, metals

The colors of the flag presumably come from the medieval arms of Hungary. The stripe design was borrowed from the French tricolor. When Hungary fought against Austrian rule in 1848, a red-white-green tricolor was hoisted. Red stands for strength, white for awareness of duty, and green for hope. The flag was introduced in 1957.

Native name: Magyaroszág
German: Ungarn
French: Hongrie
Spanish: Hungria

EUROPE

Iceland

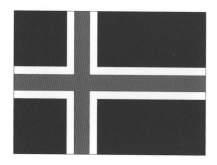

Native name: Island
German: Island
French: Islande
Spanish: Islandia

Republic of Iceland

Capital: Reykjavik
Area: 103,000 sq. km.
Population: 289,000
Language: Icelandic
Currency: Icelandic Krone

Member: NATO, OECD, OSZE, UN, WEU (associate)
Economy: fish and fish products, aluminum, medicines

The blue and white colors stand for the sea and ice, and were already immortalized in the traditional clothing of the Icelanders. Only later was the red of Denmark added, for Iceland was under Danish occupation since the 14th century. The form of the cross indicates membership in the Nordic family of peoples. Since 1944 Iceland has been an independent republic. In the same year the flag was officially introduced.

Ireland

Native name: Eire (Irish)
German: Irland
French: Irlande
Spanish: Irlanda

Republic of Ireland

Capital: Dublin
Area: 70,273 sq. km.
Population: 3,994,000
Languages: Irish, English
Currency: Euro

Member: EU, OPEC, UN
Economy: Chemical products, machines and transportation equipment

Green was always the color of the island; it stands for both the Gallic and the Norman tradition, and is also the traditional color of the Catholics. In the freedom fighting of the Irish nationalists against Great Britain, orange and white were used along with green; orange stood for the Protestant minority, the political adherents of William of Orange. White stands for unity and peaceful cooperation of the two religions.

Italy

Italian Republic

Capital: Rome
Area: 301,399 sq. km.
Population: 57,646,000
Languages: Italian,
(regionally German,
French, Slovenian)
Currency: Euro

Member: EU, G-8, NATO,
OECD, OSZE, UN, WEU
Economy: tourism, main
exports are machines,
production lines, motor
vehicles, clothing, wine

The model for the Italian flag was the French tri-color, and when Italy was under French rule from 1796 to 1814, the flag was created, apparently by Napoleon. The colors come from the uniforms of the state militia of Milan and the so-called "Italian Legion" (a local home guard of Modena). From 1861 to 1946 the arms of the royal house of Savoy adorned the flag. When Italy became a republic in 1946, the arms disappeared.

Native name: Italia (Italian)
German: Italien
French: Italie
Spanish: Italia

Latvia

Republic of Latvia

Capital: Riga
Area: 64,589 sq. km.
Population: 2,321,000
Language: Latvian
Currency: Lats
Member: EU, NATO,

OSZE, UN, WEU (asso-
ciate)
Economy: export of wood
and wood products,
metals, machines and
textiles, 77% to other
EU countries

Schon im 13. Jahrhundert wurde eine der heuti-gen Flagge ähnliche Flagge von lettischen Volks-stämmen verwendet. Die heutige Flagge wurde Ende des 19. Jahrhunderts entworfen und bis 1940 verwendet. 1940 wurde Lettland von der Sowjetunion annektiert und die Flagge war verbo-ten. Seit 1990 ist sie wieder eingeführt. Das weiße Mittelband steht für Recht, Glauben und Ehre der freien Bürger des Landes. Die rote Farbe steht für das Blut, das vergossen wurde, bis Lettland end-lich Souveränität erlangt hat.

Native name: Latvija
German: Lettland
French: Lettonie
Spanish: Letonia

EUROPE

Liechtenstein

Principality of Liechtenstein

Capital: Vaduz
Area: 160 sq. km.
Population: 34,000
Language: German
Currency: Swiss Franc

Member: OSZE, UN
Economy: exports are machines, electronic products, metal goods, glassware, ceramics

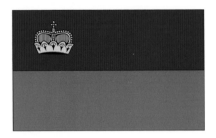

Native name: Liechtenstein
German: Liechtenstein
French: Liechtenstein
Spanish: Liechtenstein

The blue color symbolizes the sky, while the red stands for the glow of the earth and the mountains in the evening. The golden crown in the blue stripe was introduced in 1937, after it was found at the 1936 Olympic Games that the flags of Liechtenstein and Haiti were identical. The crown indicates that the land is a principality, but also symbolizes the unity of the people, princely house and government.

Lithuania

Republic of Lithuania

Capital: Vilnius
Area: 65,301 sq. km.
Population: 3,454,000
Language: Lithuanian
Currency: Litas

Member: EU, NATO, OSZE, UN, WEU (associate)
Economy: finished goods, kitchen utensils, machines, chemical products

Native name: Lietuva
German: Litauen
French: Lituanie
Spanish: Lituania

The present flag of Lithuania is a horizontal tricolor of yellow, green and red. After the country had been freed from Russian rule in 1918, after World War I, this flag was used until the country was occupied by Russia again in 1940 and the flag was banned. Only in 1989 was it introduced again. The yellow stands for the waving fields of grain, the green symbolizes the many forests and the life of the country. Red stands for Lithuania's rich flora, but also for the blood that was shed in the battles for the country's sovereignty.

Luxembourg

Grand Duchy of Luxembourg

Capital: Luxemburg
Area: 65,301sq. km.
Population: 448,000
Languages: Letzebuer-
gesch, German, French
Currency: Euro

Member: EU, NATO,
OECD, OSZE, UN, WEU
Economy: iron and steel
goods, machines and
equipment

The colors of the flag of Luxembourg are based
on the colors of the arms of a grand duke of the
13th century. At the beginning of the 19th century
Luxembourg was part of the Netherlands; thus
the similarity of design and colors of the flags.
The blue of the flag of Luxembourg is lighter than
that of the Netherlands. The flag was introduced
in its present form in 1845.

Native name: Luxembourg (French)
German: Luxemburg
Spanish: Luxemburgo

Macedonia

Republic of Macedonia

Capital: Skopje
Area: 25,713 sq. km.
Population: 2,049,000
Languages: Macedonian,
Albanian
Currency: Denar

Economy: finished
goods, drinks, tobacco,
foods, livestock

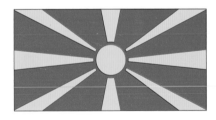

For centuries the country was under Turkish rule;
from 1913 to 1919 it belonged to Serbia, then it
became part of Yugoslavia. During the 1945-1991
Communist regime, the flag bore a red star with a
gold border on a red ground. In 1991 the flag with
a 16-cornered star was introduced, against which
Greece protested. Since 1995 the Macedonian
flag shows a yellow sun with eight rays. The sun
stands for light, life, happiness and freedom. Red
is the country's national color.

Native name: Makedonija (Macedoni-
an), Maqedonia (Albanian)
German: Mazedonien
French: Macédonie
Spanish: Macedonia

EUROPE

Malta

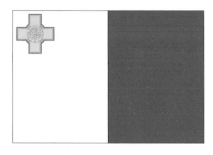

Native name: Malta (Maltese)
German: Malta
French: Malte
Spanish: Malta

Republic of Malta

Capital: Valletta
Area: 315.6 sq/km.
Population: 399,000
Languages: Maltese, English
Currency: Maltese Lira

Member: EU, OSZE, UN
Economy: machines and means of transportation, tourism

The colors of red and white are those of the Knights of St. John, which made the island their headquarters in 1530. They defended the island successfully against the Turks until 1565. As of 1800 Malta was a British fleet support point; it was strategically important during World War II. Because of the brave resistance of the Maltese, Britain awarded them the Cross of St. George in 1942; since then it has stood in the upper corner of the flag.

Moldova

Native name: Moldova
German: Moldawien
French: Moldavie
Spanish: Moldavia

Republic of Moldova

Capital: Chisinau
Area: 33,800 sq. km.
Population: 4,238,000
Languages: Moldavian, Romanian
Currency: Moldau-Leu

Member: GUS, OSZE, UN
Economy: textiles, leather goods, foods

The flag of Moldova was introduced in 1990, In 1940 Moldova was taken into the Soviet Union, and at its dissolution the separatist movement turned toward Romania. Thus the colors and eagle on the flag go back to the Romanian flag and arms. The shield shows a golden eagle with a cross in its beak and an olive branch and St. Michael's scepter in its claws. The shield portrays traditional symbols of Moldova: the ox head, rose, half-moon and star.

Monaco

Principality of Monaco

Capital: Monaco-Ville
Area: 1.95 sq. km.
Population: 33,000
Language: French
Currency: Euro

Member: OSZE, UN
Economy: highest per
capita gross national
product in the world

Monaco is the world's second smallest country (after Vatican City). The flag of two equal stripes in red and white is based on the colors of the princely Grimaldi family, which has ruled the principality for over 700 years. The flag was introduced in 1881.

Native name: Monaco
German: Monaco
Spanish: Monaco

Montenegro

Republic of Montenegro

Capital: Podgorica
Area: 13,812 sq. km.
Population: 621,000
Languages: Serbian,
Albanian
Currency: Euro

Economy: Bauxite and
iron ores, brown coal,
tobacco, salt products.
Agrarian economy with
vegetables, grain, pota-
toes, wine, citrus fruit

In May 2006, the population decided in a first plebiscite for independence from the union of Serbia and Montenegro. The Montenegrin flag, which had been accepted on July 12, 2004, goes back to the historic flag that was used until World War I, the time of the first Montenegrin independence. The golden lion on the eagle's shield is an old Montenegrin national symbol.

Native name: Crna Gora (Serbian)
German: Montenegro
French: Monténégro
Spanish: Montenegro

EUROPE

Netherlands

Native name: Nederland
German: Niederlande
French: Pays-Bas
Spanish: Paises Bajos

Kingdom of the Netherlands

Capital: Amsterdam
Area: 41,526 sq. km.
Population: 16,223,000
Language: Hollands
("Dutch")
Currency: Euro

Member: EU, NATO,
OECD, OSZE, UN, WEU
Economy: export-intensi-
ve agriculture with vege-
tables, flowers and catt-
le. 20% of the exports
go to Germany.

The Netherlands have the oldest tricolor in the world; it is known since 1579. At first the upper stripe was orange, based on the colors of Prince Willem of Orange-Nassau, who had the fight for freedom against Spain. White and blue are the colors of Nassau. In 1796 the orange stripe was changed to red to be better recognizable at sea. But orange is styill the color of the royal house, and on special days an orange triangular flag is hoisted over the tricolor.

Norway

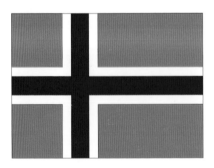

Native name: Norge
German: Norwegen
French: Norvège
Spanish: Noruega

Kingdom of Norway

Capital: Oslo
Area: 323,759 sq. km.
Population: 4,562,000
Language: Norwegian
Currency: Norwegian
Krone

Member: NATO, OECD,
OSZE, UN, WEU (asso-
ciate)
Economy: petroleum,
natural gas, petroche-
micals

From 1380 to 1814 Norway was under Danish rule. In 1814 Denmark had to give Norway to Sweden. Since 1821 Norway has had its own flag, with the blue cross added to the Danish flag. Norway had to fight a long time before its flag was also accepted by Sweden. Only in 1905 did the union with Sweden end. The cross form is typical of the Nordic lands.

Poland

Republic of Poland

Capital: Warsaw
Area: 312,685 sq. km.
Population: 39,196,000
Language: Polish
Currency: Zloty

Member: EU, NATO, OECD, OSZE, UN, WEU (associate)
Economy: Main exports are machines and electric equipment, also chemical and plastic products.

The red and white colors already appeared in military uniforms at the beginning of the 13th century. But only in 1831 did they become the national colors. The colors are also found on the national coat of arms with a silver eagle on a red background. The stripes are equally wide.

Native name: Polska
German: Polen
French: Pologne
Spanish: Polonia

Portugal

Portuguese Republic

Capital: Lisbon
Area: 92,345 sq. km.
Population: 10,444,000
Language: Portuguese
Currency: Euro

Member: EU, NATO, OECD, OSZE, UN, WEU (associate)
Economy: Portugal is one of the poorest EU countries. Exports include textiles, clothing and shoes.

The green part of the flag represents hope for a free life for all Portuguese. The red field recalls the revolution of 1910-1911, as a result of which the monarchy was abolished. The nautical instrument (armillary sphere) in the center refers to Portugal's great past as a seafaring nation.

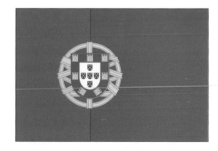

Native name: Portugal
German: Portugal
French: Portugal
Spanish: Portugal

EUROPE

Romania

Native name: Romania
German: Ruma"nien
French: Roumanie
Spanish: Rumania

Romania

Capital: Bucharest
Area: 238,391 sq. km.
leather goods and shoes
Population: 21,744,000
Language: Romanian
Currency: New Leu

Member: NATO, OSZE,
UN, WEU (associate)
Economy: Exports include
textiles, clothing and
shoes.

The Romanian tricolor goes back to the main colors of the banners of the medieval principalities of Moldavia (blue), Wallachia (yellow) and Siebenbürgen (red). Today the colors are seen as follows: Blue symbolizes the sky above the golden richness (yellow) of the land; red stands for the people's bravery. The flag was reinstated after the fall of the dictatorial regime in 1989.

Russia

Native name: Rossiya
German: Russland
French: Russie
Spanish: Rusia

Russian Federation

Capital: Moscow
Area: 238,391 sq. km.
(1st in world)
Population: 143,425,000
Language: Russian
Currency: Rubel

Member: G-8, GUS, OSZE,
UN
Economy: Over 70% of
exports are raw materials
and fuels.

The Russian flag was inspired by that of the Netherlands, where Tsar Peter was very impressed on his visit in 1697. He merely changed the order of the stripes. From 1917 to the collapse of the Soviet Union in 1991 the red flag with hammer, sickle and star was the national flag. Only since 1991 does the white-blue-red tricolor wave again. The 21 autonomous republics of the federation have their own state flags.

San Marino

Republic of San Marino

Capital: San Marino
Area: 61.2 sq. km.
Population: 28,000
Language: Italian
Currency: Euro

Member: OSZE, UN
Economy: Wine, furniture, ceramics, tourism

San Marino is one of the smallest and oldest republics in the world. The white and blue flag goes back to 1797, and the colors are based on the coat of arms, which shows three white castle towers on a blue background. The crown on top is a symbol of independence.

Native name: San Marino
German: San Marino
French: Saint Marin
Spanish: San Marino

Serbia

Republic of Serbia

Capital: Belgrade
Area: 102,173 sq. km.
Population: 8,104,000
Language: Serbian
Currency: New Dinar

Member: OSZE, UN
Economy: fin ished goods, foods, machines, apparatus

In 1918 Serbia, Croatia and Slovenia joined, and as of 1929 they were called the Kingdom of Yugoslavia. The pan-Slavic colors of the flag, red, blue and white, stand (as in the French tricolor) for freedom, equality and brotherhood. The Republics of Serbia and Montenegro have their own state flags. In 2006 Montenegro was set up as an independent state and thus separated from Serbia.

Native name: Srbija
German: Serbien
French: Serbie
Spanish: Serbia

EUROPE

Slovakia

Native name: Slovensko
German: Slowakei
French: Slovaquie
Spanish: Eslovaquia

Sloakian Republic

Capital: Bratislava
Area: 49,034 sq. km.
Population: 5,390,000
Language: Slovakian
Currency: Slovakian
Krone

Member: EU, NATO,OECD,
OSZE, UN, WEU (asso-
ciate)
Economy: Exported are
transportation, machi-
nes, among others,
means of base metals
and mineral products

In 1918 Slovakia became a part of Czechoslovakia
under the flag that the Czech Republic now uses.
In 1939 a tricolor of white, blue and red was introduced. When Czechoslovakia was dissolved in
1993, the tricolor had the Slovakian arms added
to it so as to distinguish it from the Russian flag.

Slovenia

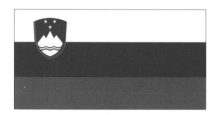

Native name: Slovenija
German: Slowenien
French: Slovénie
Spanish: Eslovenia

Republic of Sovenia

Capital: Ljubljana
Area: 20,253 sq. km.
Population: 1,995,000
Language: Slovenian
Currency: Tolar

Member: EU, NATO,
OSZE, UN, WEU (asso-
ciate)
Economy: Machinery,
textiles, chemical indu-
stry

When the Slovenians rose up against Austrian
rule at Ljubljana in 1848, a flag with three horizontal stripes of white, blue and red, the pan-Slavic
colors, was hoisted. Since Slovenia's independence in 1991 the flag has borne the arms with
the highest mountain, Triglav, its foot crossed by
two waves to symbolize the coast or the Sava and
Drava rivers.

Spain

Kingdom of Spain

Capital: Madrid
Area: 504,782 sq. km.
Population: 41,101,000
Languages: Spanish
(regional: Catalan, Gali-
cian, Basque)
Currency: Euro

Member: EU, NATO,
OECD, OSZE, UN, WEU
Economy: 67% of the
gross domestic product is
earned in services. Part-
ly-made goods,vehicles,
etc. are exported.

The colors of the Spanish flag come from the coats of arms of Castile (a golden castle on a red ground), Aragon (four red posts on a gold ground) and Navarre (a golden shirt of mail on a red ground). In the center, on the golden stripe, is the national coat of arms. The fourth field of the shield represents the province of Leon.

Native name: España (Spanish)
German: Spanien
French: Espagne

Sweden

Kingdom of Sweden

Capital: Stockholm
Area: 449,964 sq. km.
Population: 8,956,000
Language: Swedish
Currency: Swedish Krone

Member: EU, OECD,
OSZE, UN, WEU (obser-
ver)
Economy: machines,
mineral oil, foods, elec-
trotechnology

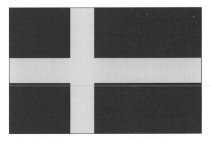

The colors of blue and yellow come from the national coat of arms used in the 14th century. The cross form indicates membership in the Nordic peoples. The flag with the horizontal yellow cross on the blue ground has existed for several centuries. It was introduced as the national flag in 1906.

Native name: Sverigge
German: Schweden
French: Suède
Spanish: Suecia

EUROPE
Switzerland

Native name: Schweiz (German), Suisse (French), Svizzera (Italian)
Spanish: Suiza
[Official name: Confederatio Helvetica, or Helvetia]

Swiss Confederation

Capital: Bern
Area: 41,285 sq. km.
Population: 7,350,000
Languages: German, French, Italian, Raetoromanisch
Currency: Swiss Franc (Schweizer Franken)

Member: OECD, OSZE, UN
Economy: This highly developed industrial land exports chemicals, machines, electronics, instruments, clocks and watches, etc.

The Swiss national flag is square and shows a white cross on a red ground. This cross stems from the Middle Ages, when many European states used a simple cross on a one-colored ground. The models were the flags of the Holy Roman Empire. In the 13th century the canton of Schwyz already had a flag with a white cross on a red ground.

The Cantons of Switzerland

Aargau

Capital: Aarau
Area: 1,404 sq. km.
Population: 568,671
Language: German

Appenzell Ausserrhoden

Capital: Herisau (seat of govt.)
Area: 243 sq. km.
Population: 52,800

Appenzell Innerrhoden

Capital: Appenzell
Area: 173 sq. km.
Population: 15,171
Language: German

Basel-Landschaft

Capital: Liestal
Area: 518 sq. km.
Population: 265,800
Language: German

Basel-Stadt

Capital: Basel
Area: 37 sq. km.
Population: 187,775
Language: German

Bern/Canton de Berne

Capital: Bern
Area: 5,959 sq. km
Population: 956,000
Languages: German, French

The Cantons of Switzerland

Freiburg (Fribourg)

Capital: Freiburg
Area: 1,671 sq. km.
Population: 251,308
Languages: German,
French

Geneva (Géneva, Genf)

Capital: Geneva
Area: 282 sq. km.
Population: 441,000
Language: French

Glarus

Capital: Glarus
Area: 685 sq. km.
Population: 38,500
Language: German

Graubünden (Grisons)

Capital: Chur
Area: 7,105 sq. km.
Population: 187,812
Language: German, Itali-
an, Ratomanisch

Jura

Capital: Delémont
Area: 838 sq. km.
Population: 69,100
Language: French

Luzern (Lucerne)

Capital: Lucerne
Area: 1,493 sq. km.
Population: 354,662
Language: German

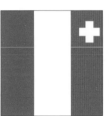

Neuenburg

Capital: Neuchâtel
Area: 803 sq. km.
Population: 167,500
Language: French

St. Gallen

Capital: St. Gallen
Area: 2,026 sq. km.
Population: 457,289
Language: German

Schaffhausen

Capital: Schaffhausen
Area: 298 sq. km.
Population: 73,900
Language: German

Schwyz

Capital: Schwyz
Area: 908 sq. km.
Population: 135,779
Language: German

The Cantons of Switzerland

Solothurn

Capital: Solothurn
Area: 791 sq. km.
Population: 247,400
Language: German

Ticino (Tessin)

Capital: Bellinzona
Area: 2,182 sq. km.
Population: 319,800
Language: Italian

Thurgau

Capital: Frauenfeld
Area: 991 sq. km.
Population: 233,912
Language: German

Unterwalden Nidwalden

Capital: Stans
Area: 276 sq. km.
Population: 39,866
Language: German

Unterwalden Obwalden

Capital: Sarnen
Area: 491 sq. km.
Population: 33,300
Language: German

Uri

Capital: Altdorf
Area: 1,077 sq. km.
Population: 35,100
Language: German

Valais (Wallis)

Capital: Sion (Sitten)
Area: 5,224 sq. km.
Population: 288,800
Languages: French, German

Vaud (Waadt)

Capital: Lausanne
Area: 3,212 sq. km.
Population: 657,700
Language: French

Zug

Capital: Zug
Area: 239 sq. km.
Population: 104,538
Language: German

Zürich

Capital: Zürich
Area: 1,729 sq. km.
Population: 1,273,278
Language: German

Ukraine

Ukraine

Capital: Kiev
Area: 603,700 sq. km.
Population: 48,356,000
Languages: Ukrainian,
Russian, minority lan-
guages
Currency: Hryvnya

Member: GUS, OSZE, UN
Economy: main exports
are iron metals, minerals
and petroleum.

The colors of the flag stand for the terrain of the
Ukraine: endless golden wheat fields under a blue
sky. In 1918 the Ukraine was briefly independent
of Russia, but in 1919 it fell under Soviet control
and remained so until 1991. During these years
the flag was banned. Since 1991 the Ukraine has
been independent, and since then the flag has
been allowed again.

Native name: Ukrajina
German: Ukraine
French: Ukraine
Spanish: Ucrania

Vatican City

State of Vatican City

Area: 0.44 sq.km
Population: 932
Languages: Latin, Ita-
lian, German (Swiss
Guard)
Currency: Euro

Member: OSZE
Economy: postage
stamps and interest on
invested money

Vatican City is the smallest state in the world and
the center of the Roman Catholic Church. The flag
consists of the colors gold and silver, which stand
for those of the keys to heaven which Jesus gave
Peter. On the white band are the keys and over
them the Pope's crown. Since 1929 this flag has
been the state flag of Vatican City.

Native name: Sancta Sedes (Latin)
German: Vatikanstadt
English: Holy See
French: Saint-siege
Spanish: Santa Sede

JIBOUTI

SOMALIA

SEYCHELLES

COMOROS

MAURITIUS

DAGASCAR   RÉUNION

Africa, the Dark Continent, extends 8,000 km from north to south and over 7,600 km from west to east. With 30.3 million square kilometers it includes one-fifth of the earth's land surface. 846 million people, 14% of the world's population, live in Africa. 41% of them belong to Islam, 48% are Christians. Africa consists of 53 independent countries recognized by the UN. The largest country is the Sudan, the smallest is Gambia. The largest city is Cairo, with 15 million Population.

Africa, because of its size and partially very difficult access, was the last continent to be colonized and exploited by the Europeans. Only after World War II did the fight of many nations for their sovereignty begin, or the ruling nations gave the nations independence stepwise, which was done relatively peacefully in most cases. With independence, most countries decided on a new form of their flags, based on traditional symbols and colors. The pan-African colors of red, yellow and green are seen on many flags; numerous coats of arms also show weapons or shields reminiscent of their ancestors.

AFRICA

AFRICA

Algeria

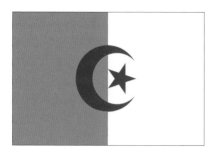

Native name: Al Jaza'ir
German: Algerien
French: Algérie
Spanish: Argelia

Democratic and Popular Republic of Algeria

Capital: Algiers
Area: 2,381,741 sq. km.
Population: 31,833,000
Language: Arabic
Currency: Algerian Dinar

Member: AU, OPEC, UN
Economy: main exports
are petroleum and hydro-
carbons (97%)

The colors of the Algerian flag stand for Islam (green), purity (white) and freedom (red). The star and crescent also stand for Islam. The horns of the moon are unusually long, for long horns are a symbol of good luck in Algeria. In 1925 the flag was first used in demonstrations against the French. Since 1962 it has been the official national flag.

Angola

Native name: Angola
German: Angola
French: Angola
Spanish: Angola

Republic of Angola

Capital: Luanda
Area: 1,246,700 sq. km.
Population: 13,522,000
Language: Portuguese
Currency: Kwanza

Member: AU, UN
Economy: 72% of the
Angolans work in agri-
culture; crude oil and its
products are the main
exports.

The red strips stands for the blood that the Angolan people shed during the Portuguese colonial rule and the subsequent war of liberation. Black represents the African continent. The half gearwheel represents the working class and industry; the machete represents the farmers and the battles. The yellow five-pointed star stands for progress.

Benin

Republic of Benin

Capital: Porto Novo
Area: 112,622 sq. km.
Population: 6,720,000
Language: French
Currency: CFA Franc

Member: AU, UN
Economy: main exports
are cotton (65%), nuts
and gold.

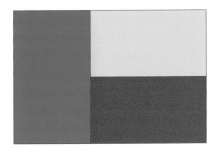

The flag shows the pan-African colors of yellow, red and green. Here yellow stands for the savannas in the north, green for palm trees in the south and red for the hilly north, but also for the blood shed by many in the fight for freedom. This flag flew from 1960 to 1975, was then replaced by the flag of the people's revolution party, and was not reintroduced until 1990.

Native name: Benin
German: Benin
Spanish: Benín

Botswana

Republic of Botswana

Capital: Gaborone
Area: 581,730 sq. km.
Population: 1,722,000
Language: English
Currency: Pula

Member: AU, UN
Economy: diamonds;
86% of the exported
goods go to Great Britain

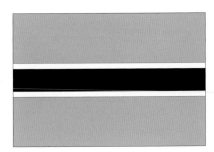

The blue takes up much space in the flag of Botswana, and that is no surprise: it stands for the sky that shall give rain, and for the water for which the population thirsts desperately. The black stripe with narrow white lines symbolizes the black majority and white minority who live in peaceful unity.

Native name: Botswana
German: Botsuana
French: Botswana
Spanish: Botsuana

AFRICA

Burkina Faso

Native name: Burkina Faso
German: Burkina Faso
Spanish: Burkina Faso

Burkina Faso

Capital: Ouagadougou
Area: 274,200 sq. km.
Population: 12,109,000
Language: French
Currency: CFA Franc

Member: AU, UN
Economy: Cotton is the
main export; also ani-
mals and animal foods

The flag of Burkina Faso shows the pan-African
colors of red, green and yellow. Red represents
the revolution, green stands for the hope of the
people to attain a revision of the government,
and for the country's natural resources. The star
stands for the leaders of the revolution; its yellow
color warns them not to forget the country's natural resources.

Burundi

Native name: Burundi (Kirundi)
German: Burundi
French: Burundi
Spanish: Burundi

Republic of Burundi

Capital: Bujumbura
Area: 27,834 sq. km.
Population: 7,206,000
Languages: Kirundi,
French
Currency: Burundi-Franc

Member: AU, UN
Economy: Burundi
exports coffee (50%),
also tea and gold.

Burundi became independent in 1962 of first
German, then Belgian rule. The flag in its present
form was introduced in 1967. Red stands for the
blood shed in the fight for independence, green
for hope and white for peace. The three stars in
the center stand for the Tutsi, Hutu and Two tribes as well as unity, work and progress.

Cameroon

Republic of Cameroon

Capital: Yaoundé
Area: 475,442 sq. km.
Population: 16,087,000
Languages: French, English
Currency: CFA Franc

Member: AU, UN
Economy: Petroleum, cotton, textile fibers, cacao, coffee and aluminum are exported.

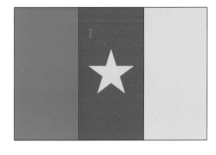

The pan-African colors of the Cameroon flag are arranged like the French tricolor. The rich vegetation and hope for well-being are expressed in the green and yellow stripes; the red stripe symbolizes the national identity. The star stands for the unity of the land, which as consisted until 1961 of French and British Cameroon. It was introduced in its present form in 1975.

Native name: Cameroun (French)
German: Kamerun
Spanish: Camerún

Cape Verde

Republic of Cape Verde

Capital: Cidade de Praia
Area: 4,036 sq. km.
Population: 470,000
Language: Portuguese
Currency: Cape Verde Escudo

Member: AU, UN
Economy: Main exports are clothing and shoes (89% of total); Portugal is the main buyer.

Cape Verde became independent of Portugal, which had owned it since the 15th century, in 1975. The blue ground of the flag symbolizes the sky and the ocean, the ten stars represent the ten islands of which the country consists. The white stripes stand for peace and harmony, while the red stripe stands for progress and the efforts that must be made.

Native name: Cabo Verde
German: Kap Verde
French: Cap-Vert
Spanish: Cabo Verde

AFRICA

Central Africa

Ldspr.: République Centrafricaine
(Französisch)
Engl.: Central African Republic
Span.: República Centroafricana

Republic of Central Africa

Capital: Bangui
Area: 622,436 sq. km.
Population: 3,881,000
Languages: Sango,
French
Currency: CFA Franc

Member: AU, UN
Economy: diamonds,
coffee, cotton and wood

Blue, white and red are the colors of the France, the former colonial power, and the pan-African colors of green, red and yellow also appear. The combination of colors stands for friendship and partnership between Europe and Africa. The golden star symbolized the country's independence, attained in 1958. The red vertical stripe also stands for the blood of all races and peoples.

Chad

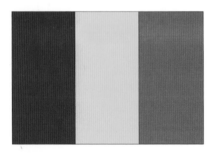

Native name: Tchad (French)
German: Tschad
Spanish: Chad

Republic of Chad

Capital: N'Djamena
Area: 1,284,000 sq. km.
Population: 8,582,000
Languages: French, Ara-
bic
Currency: CFA franc

Member: AU, UN
Economy: Cotton and
animal products are the
main exports.

The flag of Chad was influenced by the French tricolor, as the French conquered the land in 1900. The blue stripe symbolizes the sky and the water in the south, yellow is dedicated to the life-giving sun and refers to the desert in the north. Red symbolizes the emotion and dedication of the people that led them to independence in 1960.

C

Comoros

Union of the Comoros

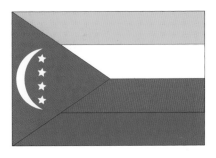

Capital: Moroni
Area: 1,862 sq. km.
Population: 600,000
Languages: Comorish,
French
Currency: Comorish Franc

Member: AU, UN
Economy: vanilla, cloves,
ylang-ylang

In 1975 the Comoros became independent of
France. Their first flag was red and bore Islamic
symbols. With the adoption of a new constitution and a new name, "Union of the Comoros", a
new flag was introduced. The green triangle and
crescent moon stand for Islam, the four stars and
four stripes for the four main islands, Moheli (yellow), Mayotte (white), Anjouan (red) and Grand
Comoro (blue).

Native name: Comores (Comorish)
German: Komoren
French: Comores
Spanish: Comoras

Congo
(Dem. Republic)

Democratic Republic of the Congo

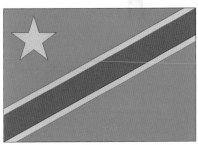

Capital: Kinshasa
Area: 2,344,885 sq. km.
Population: 53,153,000
Language: French
Currency: Congo Franc

Member: AU, UN
Economy: Main exports
are diamonds (58%),
also crude oil, copper,
cobalt and gold

The present national flag of the Democratic Republic of the Congo was introduced on February 18,
2006 after the ratification of the new constitution.
It resembles the flag that was valid from 1963
to 1971. The blue ground symbolizes peace, the
gold star unity. The red stripe stands for the blood
of martyrs and the golden frame for the riches of
the land.

Native name: République Démocrati-
que du Congo
German: Demokratische Republik
Kongo
Spanish: Républica Democrática del
Congo

Republic of the Congo

Native name: République du Congo
German: Kongo
Spanish: Congo

Republic of the Congo

Capital: Brazzaville
Area: 342,000 sq. km.
Population: 3,757,000
Language: French
Currency: CFA Franc

Member: UN
Economy: crude oil and wood are the main exports, mainly to mainland China, the Republic of Korea and the United States.

The flag of the Republic of the Congo bears the pan-African colors of red, yellow and green. Green symbolizes agriculture, yellow the mineral wealth, and red stands for independence and recalls that the blood of all races is red. The flag was first introduced in 1959, then again in 1991 after the Marxist government collapsed.

Djibouti

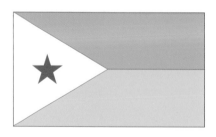

Native name: Dschibuti (Arabic), Djibouti (French)
German: Dschibuti
Spanish: Yibuti

Republic of Djibouti

Capital: Djibouti
Area: 23,200 sq. km.
Population: 705,000
Languages: Arabic, French
Currency: Djibouti Franc

Member: AU, UN
Economy: Main exports are hides, skins and other animal products

The blue stripe represents the Issa people, the green one the Afar people. These two ethnic groups make up the majority of Djibouti's population. The white triangle is to symbolize the peaceful political togetherness of the two peoples; the star stands for the unity of the people.

Egypt

Arab Republic of Egypt

Capital: Cairo
Area: 1,002,000 sq. km.
Population: 67,559,000
Language: Arabic
Currency: Egyptian
Pound

Member: AU, UN
Economy: Main exports
are fuels, oils, semi-
finished products

Red, white and black are the pan-Arabic colors,
and they also stand for the former dynasties of
the Hashemites (red), Omayades (white) and
Abbasides (black). The revolution of 1952 (which
ended the monarchy) is immortalized in the flag;
red stands for the sacrificed lives, white for the
glowing future, and black for the dark colonial
past. The white band bears the eagle of Saladin.

Native name: Misr
German: Ägypten
French: Égypte
Spanish: Egipto

Equatorial Guinea

Republic of Equatorial Guinea

Capital: Malabo
Area: 28,051 sq. km.
Population: 494,000
Language: Spanish
Currency: CFA Franc

Member: AU, UN
Economy: the main
export is petroleum,
which is
exported mainly to the
USA, Spain and China.

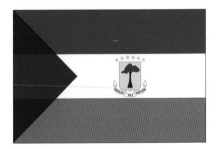

The red stripe of the flag stands for the struggle
for independence, the white for the love of peace,
and the green for the nature and resources of the
country. The blue triangle by the flagpole stands
for the ocean. The arms in the middle of the white
stripe show a kapok tree. The six stars over it
represent the mainland and the five islands.

Native name: Guinea Ecuatorial
German: Äquatorialguinea
French: Guinée équatoriale

Eritrea State of Eritrea

Capital: Asmara
Area: 121,144 sq. km.
Population: 4,390,000
Languages: Tigrinya,
Arabic
Currency: Nafka

Member: AU, UN
Economy: foods and live
animals

Native name: Ertra (Tigrinya)
German: Eritrea
French: Érythrée
Spanish: Eritrea

The three colored triangles of the flag stand for
agricultural wealth (green), marine wealth (blue)
and the blood shed during the fight for independence (red). The olive plant and the wreath stand
for the peace and prosperity of the land. In 1993
Eritrea attained independence from Ethiopia. The
present flag has been used since then.

Ethiopia Democratic Republic of Ethiopia

Capital: Addis Ababa
Area: 1,133,380 sq. km.
Population: 68,613,000
Language: Amharish
Currency: Bir

Member: AU, UN
Economy: Coffee is
exported, as are skins
and hides, oil seeds,
gold and fruit.

Native name: Ityop'iya
German: Äthiopien
French: Éthiopie
Spanish: Etiopía

The colors of the pan-African flag are based on
the Ethiopian flag: green, yellow and red. Green
stands for fruitfulness, peace and accomplish-
ment, yellow symbolizes hope, justice and equality, and red stands for work and heroism. The blue
color of the emblem stands for peace, the penta-
gram for unity, and sun rays for equality.

Gabon

Gabonese Republic

Capital: Libreville
Area: 267,667 sq. km.
Population: 1,344,000
Language: French
Currency: CFA Franc

Member: AU, UN
Economy: Main exports are petroleum, manganese and wood; the USA receives 56%, the European Union 11%.

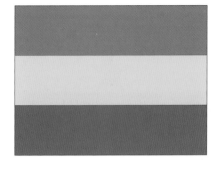

The flag of Gabon is one of the few black African flags not bearing the pan-African colors. The colors represent the geography of the land: green stands for the vast forests, yellow for the other natural resources, and blue for the ocean. Gabon became independent in 1960 after being a province of French Equatorial Africa.

Native name: Gabon
German: Gabun
French: Gabon
Spanish: Gabón

Gambia

Republic of Gambia

Capital: Banjul
Area: 11,295 sq. km.
Population: 1,421,000
Language: English
Currency: Dalasi

Member: AU, UN
Economy: Main exports are peanuts, fish and fish products.

Gambia is the smallest country on the African continent. It became independent of Great Britain in 1965, and the flag was introduced at the same time. The colors are not politically inspired: Red stands for the sun and the savannas, blue for the Gambia River and green for the forests and landscape. The narrow white stripes stand for unity, peace and freedom.

Native name: The Gambia
German: Gambia
French: Gambie
Spanish: Gambia

AFRICA

Ghana

Native name: Ghana
German: Ghana
French: Ghana
Spanish: Ghana

Republic of Ghana

Capital: Accra
Area: 238,537 sq. km. \
Population: 20,669,000
Language: English
Currency: Cedi

Member: AU, UN
Economy: Ghana exports gold, cacao and wood, especially to the Netherlands, Great Britain, France and Germany.

Ghana's flag shows the pan-African colors; red is dedicated to the freedom fighters, yellow stands for the well-being of the country and green represents the fruitful fields and forests. The black star symbolizes the freedom of Africa, The flag was introduced in 1957, when Ghana (Gold Coast) became the first British colony to gain independence.

Guinea

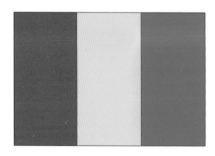

Native name: Guinea
German: Guinea
French: Guinea
Spanish: Guinea

Republic of Guinea

Capital: Conakry
Area: 245, 857 sq. km.
Population: 7,909,000
Language: French
Currency: Guinea-Franc

Member: AU, UN
Economy: aluminum and aluminum products, 21% gold

The tricolor of Guinea was introduced in 1958, when the land became independent of France. It had previously been part of French West Africa. The pan-African colors symbolize the self-sacrifice of the people during the fight for freedom (red), the sun and the natural resources (yellow), and the luxuriant vegetation of the land (green).

Guinea-Bissau

Republic of Guinea-Bissau

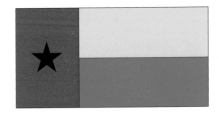

Capital: Bissau
Area: 36,125 sq. km.
Population: 1,489,000
Language: Portuguese
Currency: CFA Franc

Member: AU, UN
Economy: Cashew nuts
(96%); main buyer is
India

The flag of Guinea-Bissau was introduced in 1973, when the country became independent of Portugal and a republic was founded. The name of guinea-Bissau was chosen to differentiate it from its neighbor country. The pan-African colors symbolized the shed blood (red), sun and well-being (yellow) and rich vegetation (green). The black star stands for African unity.

Native name: Guiné-Bissau
German: Guinea-Bissau
French: Guinée-Bissau, la Guinée-
Bissau
Spanish: Guinea-Bissau

Ivory Coast

Republic of Ivory Coast, or Côte d'Ivoire

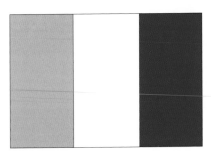

Capital: Yamousoukro
Area: 322, 462 sq. km.
Population: 16,835,000
Language: French
Currency: CFA Franc

Member: AU, UN
Economy: main exports
are cacao and cacao
products, also petroleum
products, fish and wood
products.

The order of the stripes corresponds to that of the French tricolor. The colors represent the savannas of the north and the people (orange), the rivers, peace and unity (white) and the forests of the south (green). The three colors also represent the motto of the country: Unity, discipline and work.

Native name: Côte d'Ivoire
German: Elfenbeinküste
Spanish: Costa de Marfil

AFRICA

Kenya

Republic of Kenya

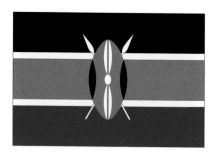

Native name: Kenya
German: Kenia
French: Kenya
Spanish: Kenia

Capital: Nairobi
Area: 580,367 sq. km.
Population: 31,916,000
Language: Swahili
Currency: Kenyan Shilling

Member: AU, UN
Economy: Kenya exports,
among others, mineral
products, raw materials,
tea, manufactured goods
and coffee

Kenya became independent in 1963 and joined
the British Commonwealth in 1964. The colors of
the flag are those of the Kenya African National
Union (KANU), which came to power with independence. Black stands for the people, red for the
blood shed in their fight for freedom, and green
for the vegetation. The white stripes stand for
unity and peace. The Masai shield and swords
recall the ancestors and stand for readiness to
defend freedom.

Lesotho

Kingdom of Lesotho

Native name: Lesotho (Sesotho)
German: Lesotho
French: Lesotho
Spanish: Lesoto

Capital: Maseru
Area: 30,355 sq. km.
Population: 1,867,000
Languages: Sesotho,
English
Currency: Loti

Member: AU, UN
Economy: Lesotho mainly
exports clothing (65%)

Since October 4, 2006, the 40th anniversary of the
country's independence, Lesotho has had a new
flag. The colors of blue, white and green stand for
rain, peace and well-being and are based on the
motto of the country. In the white stripe is a stylized Basotho hat, traditional Lesothish headgear.

Liberia

Republic of Liberia

Capital: Monrovia
Area: 97,754 sq. km.
Population: 3,374,000
Language: English
Currency: Liberian Dollar

Member: AU, UN
Economy: Liberia exports chiefly wood and natural rubber, especially to Germany, Poland and France

Liberia's flag was patterned after the American, and the colony was founded in 1816 to allow former American slaves to return to Africa. The star stands for the light of hope, freedom and peace, that radiates from the country. The blue canton symbolizes the African continent. Blue stands for freedom, white for purity and red for steadfastness.

Native name: Liberia
German: Liberia
French: Liberia
Spanish: Liberia

Libya

Libyan-Arab People's Republic

Capital: Tripoli
Area: 1,775,500 sq. km.
Population: 5,559,000
Language: Arabic
Currency: Libyan Dinar

Member: AU, OPEC, UN
Economy: 95% of Libya's exports are based on crude oil and natural gas. Italy is the main buyer.

Libya is the only country with a one-colored flag. Green is the color of Mohammed and Islam, and also stands for the "green revolution", by which, according to leader Khadafi, Libya is to be turned into a land that produces all its needed foods itself. His theories are expressed in his "Green Book".

Native name: al-Dschamahiriyya al-
     'arabiyya al-libiyya asch-scha
     'biyya al-ischtirakiyya
German: Libyen
French: Libye
Spanish: Libia

AFRICA

Madagascar

Republic of Madagascar

Native name: Madagasikara (Malagasy)
German: Madagaskar
French: Madagascar
Spanish: Madagascar

Capital: Antananarivo
Area: 587,041 sq. km.
Population: 16,894,000
Languages: Malagasy, French
Currency: Ariary

Member: AU, UN
Economy: Main exports are vanilla (24%) and crustaceans (18%).

The colors of Madagascar's flag stand for peace and freedom (white), the independence of the country (red) and hope (green). The colors of red and white are also those of the Merina upland folk of pre-colonial times, while green also represents the people of the coasts. Madagascar has been independent since 1960; the flag was introduced in 1958.

Malawi

Republic of Malawi

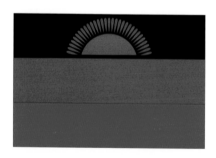

Native name: Malawi (Chichewa)
German: Malawi
French: Malawi
Spanish: Malaui

Capital: Lilongwe
Area: 118,484 sq. km.
Population: 10,962,000
Languages: Chichewa,English Currency: Malawi-Kwacha

Member: AU, UN
Economy: Tobacco (57%), tea and sugar are the main exports; the chief buyers are South Africa, the USA, Germany and Japan.

The black stripe symbolizes the peoples of Africa, while the rising sun on it stands for hope and freedom on the whole continent. The sun has 31 rays, as Malawi was the 31st African land to become independent, in 1964. The red stripe in the middle recalls the blood of African freedom fighters. Green symbolizes the forests and fields of Malawi.

Mali

Republic of Mali

Capital: Bamako
Area: 1,240,192 sq. km.
Population: 11,652,000
Language: French
Currency: CFA Franc

Member: AU, UN
Economy: gold, cotton
and cattle raising

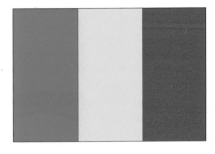

The flag of Mali shows the pan-African colors of green, yellow and red. The green embodies the nature of the land, yellow stands for the natural resources, and red symbolizes the blood shed by the people. Mali belonged to French West Africa since 1894 as the administrative district of Sudan.. Only in 1960 was the Republic of Mali founded.

Native name: Mali
German: Mali
Spanish: Mali

Morocco

Kingdom of Morocco

Capital: Rabat
Area: 458,730 sq. km.
Population: 30,113,000
Language: Arabic
Currency: Dirham

Member: UN
Economy: Clothing,
hosiery, foods and raw
materials

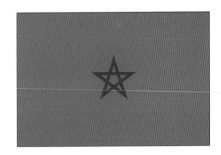

For over 300 years the presently ruling dynasty of the Alavites has used a red flag. Red is also the color of the descendants of Mohammed. The green star in the center stands for wisdom, good fortune and well-being. It was introduced in 1915, and is said to be the seal of King Solomon. The flag was officially confirmed in 1956 when the country became independent.

Native name: Al Maghrib
German: Morocco
French: Maroc
Spanish: Marruecos

AFRICA

Mauretania   Islamic Republic of Mauretania

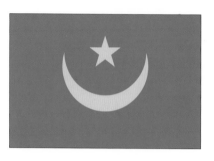

Native name: al-Djumhuriyah al-Islu-
    miyah al-Murituniyah
German: Mauretanien
French: Mauritanie
Spanish: Mauritania

Capital: Nouakchott
Area: 1,030,700 sq. km.
Population: 2,848,000
Language: Arabic
Currency: Ouguiya

Member: AU, UN
Economy: iron ore, fish
and fish products

Mauretania was a colony within French West
Africa until 1946; then it became an overseas
territory. In November 1958 the Islamic Republic
of Mauretania was proclaimed. The national flag
shows the Islamic symbols of star and crescent
moon; green is the color of the prophet Mohammed. Yellow stands for the desert and natural
resources of the country.

Mauritius   Republic of Mauritius

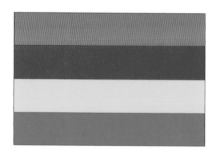

Native name: Mauritius (English)
German: Mauritius
French: Maurice
Spanish: Mauricio

Capital: Port Louis
Area: 2,040 sq. km.
Population: 1,222,000
Language: English,
French, Creole Currency:
Mauritius Rupee

Member: AU, UN
Economy: above all,
clothing, sugar cane,
fish and textile yarn are
exported.

The flag of Mauritius shows four equally wide
horizontal stripes. Red stands for the struggle for
independence, blue for the Indian Ocean, yellow
for the light of freedom and green for the fruitful land, sugar cane and flowers. Mauritius was
a French colony until 1810 and then passed to
Great Britain. The present flag was adopted in
1968 when Mauritius became independent.

Mozambique

Republic of Mozambique

Capital: Maputo
Area: 799,380 sq. km.
Population: 18,791,000
Language: Portuguese
Currency: Metical

Member: AU, UN
Economy: Aluminum and
electricity, main buyer is
South Africa

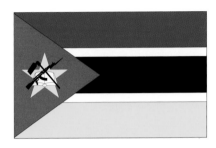

Mozambique became independent of Portugal in 1975. The colors of the flag are based on those of the Frelimo, the ruling political party. Green stands for the agricultural wealth, black for Africa and yellow for the rich natural resources of the land. The white stripes stand for justice and peace. The red triangle recalls the fight against colonialism. The elements of the arms stand for Marxism (star), education (book), watchfulness (machine gun) and agriculture (hoe).

Native name: Moçambique
German: Mosambik
French: Mozambique
Spanish: Mozambique

Namibia

Republic of Namibia

Capital: Windhoek
Area: 824,292 sq. km.
Population: 2,015,000
Language: English
Currency: Namibian
Dollar

Member: AU, UN
Economy: Diamonds are
50% of the exports,
bought mainly by South
Africa, Great Britain,
Spain, Japan and Germany

The Namibian flag was introduced in 1990 when the land became an independent republic. Until then it had been administered by South Africa (since 1961). Blue stands for the sky and precious water, red for the working people and their bravery, and green for the riches of nature. The golden sun with 12 rays in a blue field symbolizes life and energy. The white stripes stand for the peaceful co-existence of all the people in Namibia.

Native name: Namibia
German: Namibia
French: Namibie
Spanish: Namibia

Niger

Republic of Niger

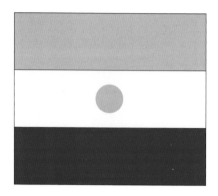

Capital: Niamey
Area: 1,267,000 sq. km.
Population: 11,762,000
Language: French
Currency: CFA Franc

Member: AU, UN
Economy: Mainly uranium, other ores, foods and live animals

Niger has a horizontal tricolor of orange, white and green. Orange stands for the Sahara and savannas, white for purity and innocence and for the Niger River, green symbolizes the rain forest and fruitful soil of the Niger Valley in the south, as well as for brotherhood. The disc stands for the sun, but also symbolizes a shield that makes the people's readiness to defend themselves clear.

Native name: Niger
German: Niger
French: Niger
Spanish: Niger

Nigeria

Federal Republic of Nigeria

Capital: Abuja
Area: 923,768 sq. km.
Population: 136,461,000
Language: English
Currency: Naira

Member: AU, OPEC, UN
Economy: The main export is petroleum (97%); 40% goes to the USA.

The two green stripes stand for the fruitfulness of the land. The white stripe stands for the great Niger River, and for unity and peace. The flag was introduced in 1960, when the country became independent. It resulted from a contest which had been announced in 1959, a year before independence.

Native name: Nigeria
German: Nigeria
French: Nigeria
Spanish: Nigera

Réunion

Departement Réunion

Capital: Saint Denis
Area: 2,512 sq. km.
Population: 753,600
Languages: French, Creole, Gujurati
Currency: Euro

Belongs to: France
Economy: Sugar, vanilla, rum and molasses are exported

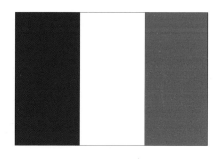

Réunion is a "Département d'outre-mer" (overseas department) since 1946. It has been French since 1642 and was originally a French penal colony for mutineers. From 1810 to 1814 it was briefly under British rule. Since it gained its present status the French flag has flown on Réunion. The population is a colorful mixture of French, Africans and Asians.

Native name: Réunion (French)
German: Réunion
Spanish: Reunión

Rwanda

Republic of Rwanda

Capital: Kigali
Area: 26,338 sq. km.
Population: 8,395,000
Languages: Kinyarwanda, French, English

Currency: Rwandan Franc
Member: AU, UN
Economy: Much coffee and tea are exported, mainly to Kenya.

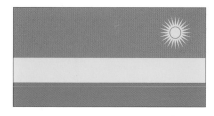

The flag of Rwanda was introduced after the end of the civil war in 2002. The colors represent the Hutu (blue), Tutsi (yellow) and Batwa (green) peoples. The flag symbolizes the peaceful life together under the sun. Blue also stands for the need of enduring peace, yellow for the natural riches, and green for the hope for well-being and use of resources.

Native name: Rwanda (Kinyarwanda)
German: Ruanda
French: Rwanda
Spanish: Ruanda

São Tomé and Príncipe

Deomcratic Republic of São Tomé and Príncipe

Capital: São Tomé
Area: 1,001 sq. km.
Population: 157,000
Language: Portuguese
Currency: Dobra

Member: AU, UN
Economy: Main export (80%) is cacao.

Native name: São Tomé e Príncipe
Greman: São Tomé und Príncipe
French: São Tomé-et-Príncipe
Spanish: Santo Tomé y Príncipe

The flag bears the pan-African colors of green, red and yellow. The green stripes stand for the forests, the yellow stripe in the middle for the island soil on which cacao grows. The red triangle is for the blood shed in battle for independence. The two stars on the yellow stripe represent the two islands of Sa~o Tomé and Pri/ncipe. The black color of the stars represents the African people.

Senegal

Republic of Senegal

Capital: Dakar
Area: 196,722 sq. km.
Population: 10,240,000
Language: French
Currency: CFA Franc

Member: AU, UN
Economy: Main export lubricants and chemical products

Native name: Sénégal
German: Senegal
Spanish: Senegal

The flag of Senegal bears the pan-African colors; the design corresponds to the French tricolor. Green stands for hope, but also for the main religions, Islam, Christianity and traditional beliefs. Yellow stands for the richness of nature and the well-being that the people can achieve through work. The red band recalls the struggle for independence, but also stands for life and social justice. The green star in the center symbolizes unity.

Seychelles

Republic of Seychelles

Capital: Victoria
Area: 454 sq. km.
Population: 84,000
Languages: Creole, Eng-
lish, French
Currency: Seychelles
Rupee

Member: AU, UN
Economy: Fish and fish
products; main buyer is
Great Britain

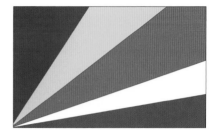

Native name: Seychelles (English)
German: Seychellen
French: Seychelles
Spanish: Seychelles

Since independence cam in 1976 there have been three different flags on the Seychelles. The five colors of the present flag stand for the two largest parties: blue and white are the Democratic Party colors; red, white and green are those of the Seychelles Peoples United Party (SPUP). Blue also stands for sky and seas, yellow for the sun, red for work, white for harmony and social justice, and green for the environment. The present flag was introduced in 1996.

Sierra Leone

Republic of Sierra Leone

Capital: Freetown
Area: 71,740 sq. km.
Population: 5,337,000
Language: English
Currency: Leone

Member: AU, UN
Economy: 90% of the
exports are diamonds,
there are also cacao and
coffee.

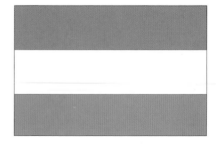

Native name: Sierra Leone
German: Sierra Leone
French: Sierra Leone
Spanish: Sierra Leone

Sierra Leone has been independent of Great Britain since 1961. The colors of its flag come from its arms, developed in London. Green stands for agriculture, natural beauty and mountains. The white stripe symbolizes unity, peace and justice. The blue stripe stands for the ocean and the hope that Freetown, the only natural harbor of the country, will continue to give fine service for foreign trade and economic development.

AFRICA

Somalia

Republic of Somalia

Native name: Somaaliya
German: Somalia
French: Somalie
Spanish: Somalia

Capital: Mogadishu
Area: 637,657 sq. km.
Population: 9,626,000
Language: Somali
Currency: Somalian Shilling

Member: AU, UN
Economy: cattle raising, hides, skins, fruit and fish

The blue color comes from the United Nations flag. The white star symbolizes the freedom of Africa and the African peoples. The five points stand for the five regions in which the Somali people now live: Somalia, which was made of the former British and Italian Somaliland in 1960, plus Djibouti, Ethiopia and Kenya. The flag was already introduced in 1954 by the former Italian Somaliland and taken over in 1960 with the independence.

South Africa

Republic of South Africa

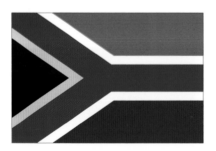

Native name: South Africa (English)
German: Su..dafrika
French: Afrique du Sud
Spanish: Suda/frica

Capital: Pretoria
Area: 1,219,000 sq. km.
Population: 47,850,700
Languages: English, Afrikaans, Ndebele, North and South Sotho, Setswana, Swati, Tsonga, Venda, Xhosa, Zulu
Currency: Rand
Member: AU, UN
Economy: Precious stones, pearls, metals and mineral materials are exported.

The colorful South African flag was introduced in 1994 when the Apartheid regime ended. Yellow, black and green are the colors of the African National Congress, which
Came to power that year. Red, white and blue are the traditional colors of the Boer republics and are based on the Netherlands flag. The lying Y stands for the coming together of the formerly hostile groups and embodies the hope for progress and a unified path into the future.

St. Helena

St. Helena

Capital: Jamestown
Area: 410 sq. km.
Population: 4,647
Language: English
Currency: British Pound

Belongs to: Great Britain
Economy: Chiefly fish
and coffee

St. Helena was captured from Portugal in 1502
and taken by the Netherlands in 1600, who sold
it to Great Britain in 1650. Since 1834 it has been
a British colony, and has the status of a United
Kingdom Overseas Territory. St. Helena is administered by a governor, and it has it own 14-mem-
ber parliament. The flag is dark blue and shows
the Union Jack in the union plus the coat of arms
with a British sailing ship.

Native name: Saint Helena
German: St. Helena
French: Sainte-Hélène
Spanish: Santa Helena

Sudan

Republic of Sudan

Capital: Khartoum
Area: 2,508,813 sq. km.
Population: 33,546,000
Language: Arabic
Currency: Sudanese Dinar

Member: AU, UN
Economy: petroleum,
meat and live animals

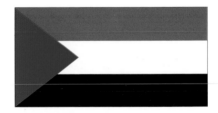

Until 1956 the land was ruled by Egypt and Great
Britain; the Republic of Sudan was proclaimed in
1968, and in the same year there was a competition for the design of the new flag, which was
introduced in 1970. Red stands for revolution,
socialism and progress, white for light, peace and
optimism, while black stands for Africa. The green
triangle at the hoist symbolizes Islam and well-
being.

Native name: As-Sudan
German: Sudan
French: Soudan
Spanish: Sudán

Swaziland

Kingdom of Swaziland

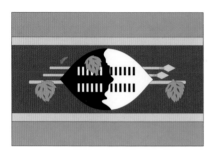

Capital: Mbabane
Area: 17,363 sq. km.
Population: 1,169,000
Languages: Siswati,
English
Currency: Lilangeni

Member: AU, UN
Economy: fruits and fruit
concentrates, wood and
wood products

Native name: Swaziland (English)
German: Swasiland
French: Swaziland
Spanish: Suazilandia

Swaziland was a British protectorate, ruled by King Mswati III, until 1968. The flag was already designed in 1954 and based on a flag that was given to the Swazi troops of the British Africa Corps by King Sobhuza II in 1941. It was introduced only in 1967. Blue stands for peace, yellow for natural resources. The red central stripe recalls past battles. The Swazi shield stands for the Swazi warriors' readiness to fight.

Tanzania

United Republic of Tanzania

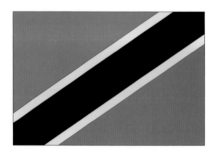

Capital: Dodoma
Area: 945,087 sq. km.
Population: 35,889,000
Languages: Swahili,
English
Currency: Tanzanian
Shilling

Member: AU, UN
Economy: The main
export goods are cashew
nuts,coffee, minerals,
tobacco and cotton.

Native name: Tanzania (Swahili)
German: Tansania
French: Tanzanie
Spanish: Tanzania

The present-day Tanzania is a union of Tanganyika and Zanzibar formed in 1964. The traditional flag colors of the two lands are united in the flag: Green, yellow and black represent Tanganyika, blue, black and green Zanzibar. Green stands for the land, black for the people and Africa, blue for the ocean and Zanzibar, and yellow for the mineral wealth in Tanzania.

Togo

Republic of Togo

Capital: Lomé
Area: 56,785 sq. km.
Population: 4,861,000
Languages: French, Ewe,
Kabyé Currency: CFA
Franc

Member: AU, UN
Economy: Manufactured
goods, fertilizers and
mineral raw materials,
foods and live animals
are exported.

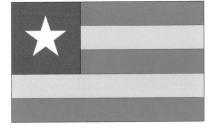

Togo was a German protectorate until 1918; then it was divided between France and Great Britain, later administered under UN oversight, and became autonomous in 1955. In 1960 it became independent and received the name of Togo and the flag. The five-pointed star symbolizes the five regions of the country, green stands for agriculture, yellow for natural resources, red for blood and white for purity and hope.

Native name: République Togolaise
   (French)
German: Togo
English: Togo
Spanish: Togo

Tunisia

Tunisian Republic

Capital: Tunis
Area: 163,610 sq. km.
Population: 9,895,000
Language: Arabic
Currency: Tunisian Dinar

Member: AU, UN
Economy: clothing, knit-
ted goods, shoes and oil

Until 1881 Tunisia was part of the Ottoman Empire, whose traditional imperial color was red. The crescent moon and star are traditional symbols of Islam. The Tunisian flag greatly resembles the Turkish flag. The red also stands for the blood shed in the fight for freedom. In 1835 the crescent moon and star were placed in a white circle which symbolizes the sun and the unity of the country.

Native name: Tunis
German: Tunesien
French: Tunisie
Spanish: Túnez

AFRICA

Uganda

Republic of Uganda

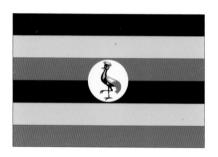

Native name: Uganda (English)
German: Uganda
French: Ouganda
Spanish: Uganda

Capital: Kampala
Area: 241,548 sq. km.
Population: 25,280,000
Languages: Swahili, English

Currency: Ugandan Shilling
Member: AU, UN
Economy: Main exports are coffee, tea and cotton, 26% going to EU lands.

Uganda became independent of Great Britain in 1962. Since them this three-colored flag with a crane in the center waves over the land. It is based on the flag of the victorious party (UPC) and was made the national flag with the crane added. The colors symbolize Africa and its Population (black), the sun (yellow) and the friendship of man (red).

Western Sahara

Democratic Arabic Republic of Sahara

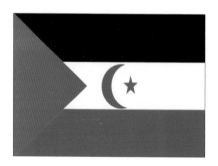

Native name: Al-Sahra' al-Garbiyyah
German: Westsahara
French: Sahara occidental
Spanish: Sa/hara Occidental

Capital: El-Aujún
Area: 266,001 sq. km.
Population: 373,000
Language: Arabic
Currency: Sahuraui-Peseta (Moroccan dirham)

Belongs to: Strives for independence.
Economy: Chiefly agrarian; great poverty prevails.

Since 1976 Western Sahara has been a republic recognized by 60 nations worldwide. The country declared itself independent of Morocco, but Morocco did not recognize this. The UN suggested a referendum on the autonomy of the country, but this was postponed. The Western Saharan flag uses the pan-Arabic colors. Red is for the shed blood, black for the colonial rule, white for peace and green for progress and Islam.

Zambia

Republic of Zambia

Capital: Lusaka
Area: 752,614 sq.km
Population: 10,403,000
Language: English
Currency: Kwacha

Member: AU, UN
Economy: Copper; main
buyers are Great Britain,
South Africa and Swit-
zerland

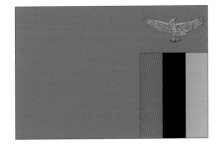

The big green field of the flag symbolizes the natural wealth of the country. At the outer end are vertical red, black and orange stripes. They stand for the fight for freedom (red), the Zambian people (black) and the copper deposits (orange). The flying eagle symbolizes the will to freedom and the ability of the people to deal with all problems.

Native name: Zambia
German: Sambia
French: Zambie
Spanish: Zambia

Zimbabwe

Republic of Zimbabwe

Capital: Harare
Area: 390,757 sq. km.
Population: 13,102,000
Language: English
Currency: Zimbabwe
Dollar

Member: AU, UN
Economy: tobacco, flo-
wers, sugar, minerals
and industrial goods

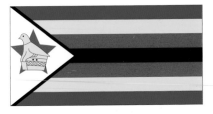

The green stripes of the flag stand for vegetation and agriculture, the yellow for the mineral wealth, the red for the blood shed during the fight for independence. The black stripe represents Africa, the Dark Continent. The red star symbolizes the socialistic state philosophy. The "Great Zimbabwe Bird" is the national emblem.

Native name: Zimbabwe
German: Simbabwe
French: Zimbabwe
Spanish: Zimbabue

America consists of the two continents of North and South America, linked by the isthmus of Central America. The two continents cover 42 million square kilometers, with 17.8 million sq. km. making up South America, 10 million sq. km. Canada and 9.6 million sq. km. the United States.

The two continents consist of 35 independent states recognized by the UN and many small lands and islands that are administered by other countries. The largest city is Mexico City, with 8.5 million Population.

After America had been found by Columbus, settlers from Europe came to it. North America was settled mainly by Britons, Central and South America by Spaniards and Portuguese, which has shaped their cultures and languages. During the conquest and settlement Native Americans, the original inhabitants, were decimated and numerous groups completely wiped out.

The most influential and heavily populated land is the United States of America, consisting of 50 states. The flag of the USA, the Stars and Stripes, was the model for numerous other flags.

The countries of Central America look back on colonization and wars of liberation. Many national flags were inspired by the French tricolor.

South America consists of 13 independent countries, the largest being Brazil, the smallest Suriname.

AMERICA

Anguilla

Native name: Anguilla
German: Anguilla
French: Anguilla
Spanish: Anguila

Anguilla

Capital: The Valley
Area: 96 sq. km.
Population: 11,430
Language: English
Currency: East Caribbean
Dollar

Belongs to: Great Britain
Economy: Tourism brings
in the most money; fish,
fruit, salt and rum are
exported

Anguilla,since 1650 a British colony consisting of the islands of Anguilla and Sombrero, was proclaimed a republic in 1967. Considerations about a union with St. Kitts and Nevis followed. Since 1980, Anguilla has been a „United Kingdom Overseas Territory" with a high degree of self-government. The flag is dark blue, bears the Union Jack in the canton and the coat of arms to its right, consisting of three dolphins that symbolize unity. The light blue stripe stands for the Caribbean.

Antigua and Barbuda

Native name: Antigua and Barbuda
German: Antigua und Barbuda
French: Antiqua-et-Barbuda
Spanish: Antigua y Barbuda

Antigua and Barbuda

Capital: St. John's
Area: 96 sq. km.
Population: 79,000
Language: English
Currency: East Caribbean
Dollar

Member: CARICOM, OAS,
UN
Economy: machines,
petroleum, manufactured
goods

The sun stands for a new era after independence in 1967. The black field symbolizes the African origin of the population. Blue stands for hope, white for sand. The wedge as a whole stands for the English word "Victory" over colonialism. The colors in it represent sun, sea and sand. The red triangles at left and right symbolize the energy of the population.

Argentina

Argentine Republic

Capital: Buenos Aires
Area: 2,780,403 sq. km.
Population: 36,772,000
Language: Spanish
Currency: Argentine Peso

Member: OAS, UN
Economy: mining pro-
ducts, fuels, foods

Blue and white represent the sky and the snow of the Andes. The colors also have political origins and go back 1810. The uniforms of the soldiers of General Belgrano, one of the leaders of the war for independence against Spain, were decorated in blue and white. In 1816 the flag with the three stripes, and in 1918 the sun, the national symbol, was added.

Native name: Argentina
German: Argentinien
French: Argentine

Aruba

Aruba

Capital: Oranjestad
Area: 193 sq. km.
Population: 93,333
Languages: Dutch,
Papiamento, Spanish,

English Currency: Aruban
Florin
Belongs to: Netherlands
Economy: Animals and
animal products, machi-
nes and electric devices
are exported

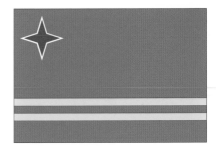

Aruba belonged to the Netherlands Antilles until 1986. Today it is an autonomous part of the Netherlands, with a parliament, governor and chief of government. It was discovered by the Spaniards in 1499 and has been ruled by the Netherlands since 1636. The flag of Aruba is UN blue; the two yellow stripes in the lower part symbolize the rainflower, the sun and tourism. Blue stands for the sky and the sea. The star represents Aruba and the four compass points from which settlers came.

Native name: Aruba (Dutch)
German: Aruba
French: Aruba
Spanish: Aruba

AMERICA

Bahamas

Commonwealth of the Bahamas

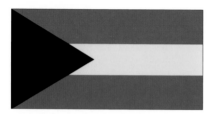

Capital: Nassau
Area: 13,939 sq. km.
Population: 271,000
Language: English
Currency: Bahaman
Dollar

Member: CARICOM, OAS,
UN
Economy: Manufactured
goods, machines, mine-
ral oils

Native name: The Bahamas
German: Bahamas
French: Bahamas
Spanish: Bahamas

The blue stripes point to the treasures of the sea that surrounds the Bahamas. The yellow stripe stands for the resources and the endless sandy beaches. The triangle at the hoist stands for the spirit and determination of the population, the color black reflects the joy of living and strength of the people. The flag was created in a contest and introduced in 1973.

Barbados

Barbados

Capital: Bridgetown
Area: 430 sq. km.
Population: 271,000
Language: English
Currency: Barbados Dol-
lar

Member: CARICOM, OAS,
UN
Economy: Foods, live
animals, petroleum, che-
micals

Native name: Barbados
German: Barbados
French: Barbados
Spanish: Barbados

The blue side stripes stand for the ocean and the sky, the golden middle stripe for the beaches of the Caribbean island. The trident recalls Neptune and shows the people's close contact with the sea. The fact that the shaft is broken off expresses the break with the colonial past. The flag was first hoisted in 1996, when Barbados attained independence.

Belize

Belize

Capital: Belmopan
Area: 22,965 sq.cm.
Population: 274,000
Language: English
Currency: Belize Dollar

Member: CARICOM, OAS, UN
Economy: agricultural products, mainly fish and fruit

Blue and white are the colors of the United People's Party, while red is the color of the Democratic Party. In the middle of the flag is the national coat of arms, surrounded by a wreath of 50 leaves, recalling that the fight for independence began in that year. The arms have existed since 1907, when Belize was still British Honduras.

Native name: Belize
German: Belize
French: Belize
Spanish: Belice

Bermuda

Bermuda

Capital: Hamilton
Area: 43 sq. km.
Population: 65,545
Languages: English, Portuguese
Currency: Bermuda Dollar

Belongs to: Great Britain
Economy: Tourism and finance

Bermuda consists of some 360 islands, only over twenty of which are inhabited. The name came from the Spanish explorer Juan de Bermúdez, who discovered it in 1503. It has been a British colony since 1648 and now has United Kingdom Overseas Territory status, with self-government, since 1968. It is governed by a governor, head of government and house of representatives. The flag shows the Union Jack in the union, and the coat of arms with a lion holding a shield with a shipwreck.

Native name: Bermuda (English)
German: Bermuda
French: Bermudes
Spanish: Bermudas

Bolivia

Native name: Bolivia (Spanish)
German: Bolivien
English: Bolivia
French: Bolivie

Republic of Bolivia

Capital: Sucre
Administrative: La Paz
Area: 1,098,581 sq. km.
Population: 8,814,000
Languages: Spanish,
Quechua, Aimará
Currency: Boliviano

Member: OAS, UN
Economy: Oil and other
fuels, soy, soy meal,
zinc, tin

The red stripe symbolizes the love of homeland and bravery of the soldiers who fought for independence. The yellow stripe in the middle stands for the rich natural resources of the land and represents the Inca people. Green symbolized the fruitfulness of the land, as well as hope. The arms show the mountain Potosi, a llama, a breadfruit tree and various weapons and banners.

Brasil

Native name: Brasil
German: Brasilien
English: Brazil
French: Brésil
Spanish: Brasil

Federative Republic of Brasil

Capital: Brasilia
Area: 8,547,404 sq. km.
Population: 176,596,000
Language: Portuguese
Currency: Real

Member: OAS, UN
Economy: metals and
metal products, soy,
meat, petroleum

The green color stands for the forests and the wealth of plants. Yellow indicates the wealth of natural resources and minerals. The yellow diamond on a green ground has been on the Brazilian flag since 1822. The constellation of stars in the middle shows the sky over Rio de Janeiro as it was on the day the republic was proclaimed. Every star stands for a federal state, the number of which was last corrected in 1992.

British Virgin Islands

Capital: Road Town
Area: 153 sq. km.
Population: 21,000
Language: English
Currency: U.S. Dollar

Belongs to: Great Britain
Economy: Tourism is most profitable; fruit, rum and fish are exported.

British Virgin Islands

The British Virgin Islands consist of 40 islands, the largest being Tortola, Anegada, Virgin Gorda and Jost Van Dyke. The islands have been British since 1672 and a British colony since 1872. Today they are a United Kingdom Overseas Territory with self-government, a constitution and a parliament. The flag is dark blue, with the Union Jack in the union. The islands' coat of arms portrays St. Ursula.

Native name: British Virgin Islands
German: Britische Jungferninseln
French: Iles Vierges britanniques
Spanish: Islas Vírgenes Británicas

Canada

Capital: Ottawa
Area: 9,984,670 sq. km.
Population: 31,630,000
Languages: English,French

Currency: Canadian Dollar
Member: G-8, NAFTA, NATO, OAS, OECD, OSZE, UN
Economy: Machines, automobiles and parts, energy, wood

Canada

The Canadian flag with the maple leaf is unmistakable. The maple leaf has been the country's national symbol since the mid-19th century. The red stripes at left and right stand for the Atlantic and Pacific Oceans that border Canada to the east and west. The red color recalls the sacrifices of World War I. The broad white stripe in the middle symbolizes the vast snowy areas in the north. The flag was introduced in 1965.

Native name: Canada (Engflish/ French)
German: Kanada
Spanish: Canadá

AMERICA

Cayman Islands

Native name: Cayman Islands
German: Kaimaninseln
French: Iles Cayman
Spanish: Islas Caima/n

Cayman Islands

Capital: George Town
Area: 259 sq. km.
Population: 41,000
Language: English
Currency: Cayman Dollar

Belongs to: Great Britain
Economy: Tourism and
financial services

The Cayman Islands consist of Grand Cayman, Cayman Brac and Little Cayman. They have been British since 1670 and have the status of a United Kingdom Overseas Territory with self-government since 1962. The population consists of blacks and mulattos plus about 1600 whites. The flag shows the Union Jack in the union, and on the right side the coat of arms that has existed since 1958. It shows three stars for the three islands, a lion, and blue wave lines. The turtle and bananas stand for the flora and fauna.

Chile

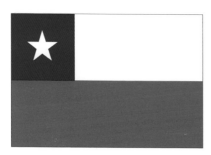

Native name: Chile
German: Chile
French: Chili

Republic of Chile

Capital: Santiago de
Chile
Area: 756,096 sq. km.
Population: 15,774,000
Language: Spanish
Currency: Chilean Peso

Member: OAS, UN
Economy:
Mining,industrial produc-
tion, fishing, agriculture.

The white stripe stands for the snow of the Andes, the red stripe for the blood shed by heroes in the fight for freedom. The blue square symbolizes the sky; the white star is to lead the way to a future of progress. The five points of the star stand for the original five provinces of the country. The flag was introduced when the country became independent in 1817.

Columbia

Republic of Columbia

Capital: Bogota
Area: 1,141,748 sq. km.
Population: 44,584,000
Language: Spanish
Currency: Colombian
Peso

Member: CARICOM
(observer), OAS, UN
Economy: Petroleum,
industrial products, coal,
agriculture

The colors of the flag were already used by the
Republic of Greater Colombia from 1819 to 1834.
That country was divided into Colombia, Venezuela and Ecuador, and Colombia took over the flag.
The yellow stripe symbolizes the golden beaches
of Latin America, separated by the ocean (blue)
from the bloody colonial power of Spain (red).
Today the colors are seen differently; they stand
for freedom, justice and courage.

Native name: Colombia
German: Kolumbien
French: Colombie

Costa Rica

Republic of Costa Rica

Capital: San José
Area: 51,100 sq. km.
Population: 4,005,000
Language: Spanish
Currency: Costa Rican
Colon

Member: OAS, UN
Economy: Electronics,
medicinal technology,
bananas, pineapple,
coffee

The white and blue colors come from the flag of
the Central American Federation. The red stripe
was added in 1848 at the instigation of the Federation president's wife. She subscribed to the revo-
lutionary ideals of liberty, equality and fraternity.
The oval coat of arms shows the three highest
mountains of the land amid the blue ocean. Seven
stars in the sky indicate the seven provinces.

Native name: Costa Rica
German: Costa Rica
French: Costa Rica

AMERICA

Cuba

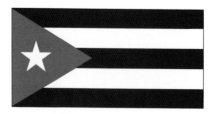

Native name: Cuba
German: Kuba
French: Cuba

Republic of Cuba

Capital: Havana
Area: 110,860 sq. km.
Population: 11,326,000
Language: Spanish
Currency: Cuban Peso

Member: OAS (suspended), UN
Economy: Sugar, nickel, fruit, tobacco

The Cuban flag is oriented to the Stars and Stripes of the USA. The white star on the red triangle symbolizes Cuba, which once wanted connections with the USA. The red triangle at the hoist embodies the three basic elements of the republic: liberty, equality and fraternity. The three blue stripes stand for the three provinces of which Cuba consisted at its independence. The two white stripes symbolize the purity of the revolution.

Dominica

Native name: Dominica
German: Dominica
French: Domonique
Spanish: Domonica

Dominica

Capital: Roseau
Area: 751 sq. km.
Population: 71,000
Language: English
Currency: East Caribbean Dollar

Member: CARICOM, OAS, UN
Economy: Soap, bananas, exported to Jamaica and Great Britain

Green stands for the vegetation of the land, the cross symbolizes the Christian faith of the population, the three colors indicate the Trinity. Yellow also stands for the sun, black for the soil and white for the waters. The arms were granted by Great Britain in 1961 and show the Sisserou parrot, the national bird. It is surrounded by ten stars that stand for the ten communities.

Dominican Republic

Dominican Republic

Capital: Santo Domingo
Area: 48,422 sq. km.
Population: 8,739,000
Language: Spanish
Currency: Dominican Peso

Member: CARICOM (observer), OAS, UN
Economy: Nickel, raw sugar, cacao, tobacco

The blue rectangles stand for freedom, the red ones recall the courage of the state's founders. The white cross symbolizes Christian salvation as well as the self-sacrifice of the population during the fight for freedom. The coat of arms repeats the flag's colors in the form of a shield and shows a bible open to the Gospel of St. John, a symbol of the Trinitarians who led the fight for freedom against Haiti.

Native name: La Dominicana
German: Dominikanische Republik
French: République dominicaine

Ecuador

Republic of Ecuador

Capital: Quito
Area: 256,370 sq. km.
Population: 13,008,000
Language: Spanish
Currency: U.S. Dollar, Sucre

Member: OAS, UN
Economy: Petroleum, industrial products, bananas, flowers, crabs

The colors of the Ecuadorean flag are based on those of the Republic of Greater Colombia, which Ecuador joined in 1822. The yellow stripe symbolizes the sun and the natural resources, the blue stripe stands for the sky and sea, and the red stripe for courage and is dedicated to those who shed their blood in the fight for freedom. The arms show the mouth of the Guaya River before the volcano Chimborazo.

Native name: Ecuador
German: Ecuador
French: Équateur

AMERICA

El Salvador

Republic of El Salvador

Native name: El Salvador
German: El Salvador
French: Salvador, l'El Salvador

Capital: San Salvador
Area: 21,041 sq. km.
Population: 6,533,000
Language: Spanish
Currency: El Salvador
Colon

Member: OAS, UN
Economy: coffee is 1/3
of the total exports

The flag colors of El Salvador go back to the flag of the Central American Federation, which existed from 1823 to 1838. The two blue stripes symbolize the ocean and Caribbean Sea (although El Salvador is only on the Pacific). The white middle stripe stands for peace. In the middle stripe is the coat of arms, consisting of a triangular shield,, representing the judicial, legislative and executive branches. Five volcanoes and five flags stand for the five regions.

Falkland Islands

Falkland Islands

Native name: Falkland Islands
German: Falkland-Inseln
French: Iles Falkland
Spanish: Islas Malvinas

Capital: Stanley
Area: 21,173 sq.km. and 200 small islands Population: 2,913 and 1,500 British soldiers
Language: English

Currency: Falkland Pound
Belongs to: Great Britain
Economy: Raising animals for meat, skin and fleece

The Falkland Islands were a British colony since 1838. Since 1985 their status has been a United Kingdom Overseas Territory. The flag is dark blue, with the Union Jack in the union, plus the arms of the islands, a white circle showing a shield. In the upper part is a ram, indicating the significance of wool. The waved stripes portray the ocean, the ship is the "Desire" on which the discoverers of the islands sailed in 1592.

French-Guyana

French-Guyana

Capital: Cayenne
Area: 83,534 sq. km.
Population: 173,000
Languages: French, Creole
Currency: Euro

Belongs to: France
Economy: Rum, shrimp, wood, gold and textiles are exported.

The first French settled in the land in 1604, and in 1817 the land became a French possession. In 1946 it was made an Overseas Departement of France and gained limited self-government. At the end of the 19th century Brazil made a claim on the area, and the border dispute was ended in favor of French only in 1900. The flag is the French Tricolor.

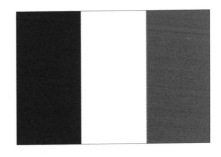

Native name: Guyane (French)
German: Französisch-Guyana
French: Guyane franç3aise
Spanish: Guayana Francesa

Grenada

Grenada

Capital: St. George's
Area: 344.5 sq. km.
Population: 105,000
Language: English
Currency: East Caribbean Dollar

Member: CARICOM, OAS, UN
Economy: Electronic components, nutmeg

Grenada is also called the spice island, which shows up on the flag. The green triangles stand for the rich vegetation, the nutmeg indicates the island's most important trade goods. The yellow triangles symbolize the island's sunny situation and the people's hearty spirit. The seven stars stand for the seven administrative districts, the red frame for the unity of the people. The flag was introduced on the day of independence in 1974.

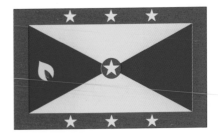

Native name: Grenada
German: Grenada
French: Grenade
Spanish: Granada

AMERICA

Guadeloupe

Native name: Guadeloupe (French)
German: Guadeloupe
Spanish: Guadalupe

Guadeloupe

Capital: Basse-Terre
Area: 1,705 sq. km.
Population: 435,000
Languages: French,Creole
Currency: Euro

Belongs to: France
Economy: Tourism is the
chief source of income;
bananas, sugar and rum
are exported.

Guadeloupe has belonged to France since 1635. The land consists of nine inhabited islands. The population is 77% Mulatto, 10% Black, 10% Creole and 120,000 Indians. Since 1946 Guadeloupe has been a "Département d'outre-mer" with its own parliament and a prefect in the government. Like the other overseas departements, Guadeloupe uses the French flag. There is also a flag of Guadeloupe that may be flown beside the Tricolor.

Guatemala

Native name: Guatemala
German: Guatemala
French: Guatemala

Republic of Guatemala

Capital: Guatemala
Area: 108,889 sq. km.
Population: 12,307,000
Language: Spanish
Currency: Quetzal

Member: OAS, UN
Economy: Clothing, coffee, bananas, sugar, and petroleum.

The colors of the flag come from those of the Central American Federation. In addition, the blue stripes at the left and right stand for the Atlantic and Pacific Oceans on which Guatemala fronts. Blue also stands for justice and white for righteousness. The arms show guns, bayonets and swords, but also the Quetzal, a rare bird that can survive only in freedom.

Guyana

Co-operative Republic of Guyana

Capital: Georgetown
Area: 214,969 sq. km.
Population: 796,000
Language: English
Currency: Guyana Dollar

Member: CARICOM, OAS, UN
Economy: Gold, sugar, rice, shrimp

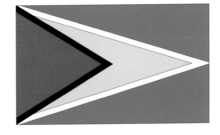

Guyana was a British colony, called British Guiana, until 1966. The flag was introduced in 1966 and had strong color symbolism. Green refers to the agriculture and woodlands, the golden arrow stands for the rich natural resources, the white rim for the waters. The red triangle stands for the people's energy in building an independent nation. The black stripe expresses the resistant power of the people.

Native name: Guyana
German: Guyana
French: Guyana
Spanish: Guyana

Haiti

Republic of Haiti

Capital: Port-au-Prince
Area: 27,750 sq. km.
Population: 8,440,000
Languages: French, Creole
Currency: Gourde

Member: CARICOM, OAS, UN
Economy: manufactured goods and coffee

The blue stripe stands for the people, the red for the blood shed in the fight for freedom. Haiti declared its freedom from the French occupiers in 1804. The blue-white-red Tricolore flown until then was redesigned without the white stripe, which recalled the occupation. Since 1840 the stripes have been horizontal. The two stripes also symbolize the unity of blacks and mulattoes today.

Native name: Haïti (French)
German: Haiti
Spanish: Haiti

AMERICA

Honduras

Republic of Honduras

Native name: Honduras
German: Honduras
French: Honduras

Capital: Tegucigalpa
Area: 122,492 sq. km.
Population: 6,969,000
Language: Spanish
Currency: Lempira

Member: OAS, UN
Economy: shellfish, coffee, bananas

Honduras was a member of the Central American Federation from its founding in 1823 to its dissolution in 1838. The present flag scarcely differs from that of the Federation. The blue stripes symbolize the two oceans on which the land fronts; the white middle stripe stands for the peace in the country. The five stars were added in 1866 and stand for the five founding states: Guatemala, Nicaragua, Honduras, Costa Rica and El Salvador.

Jamaica

Jamaica

Native name: Jamaica
German: Jamaika
French: Jamaïque
Spanish: Jamaica

Capital: Kingston
Area: 10,991 sq. km.
Population: 2,643,000
Language: English
Currency: Jamaican
Dollar

Member: CARICOM, OAS, UN
Economy: foods, raw materials, drinks, tobacco

The Jamaican flag was officially introduced on the occasion of the country's independence on August 6, 1962. It was designed by a committee of the Jamaican legislature. Black stands for the difficult past and the tests that the people still have to pass. Green symbolizes vegetation and agriculture, but also hope. The golden diagonal cross symbolizes the sun and the country's natural riches.

Mexico

United Mexican States

Capital: Mexico City
Area: 1,953,162 sq. km.
Population: 106,202,903
Language: Spanish
Currency: Mexican Peso

Member: CARICOM
(observer), NAFTA, OAS,
OECD, UN

The green stripe at the hoist stands for independence, the white in the center for the purity
of the (Catholic) faith, and the red stripe at right
represents the equality (of blood) of all races and
people in the country. The arms are based on the
mythology of the Aztecs: Eagle and snake stand
for sun and earth and symbolize the blend of
cosmic powers. The flag has existed in this form
since 1968.

Native name: México
German: Mexiko
France: Mexique

Montserrat

Montserrat

Capital: Brades
Area: 102 sq. km.
Population: 4,482
Language: English
Currency: East Caribbean
Dollar

Belongs to: Great Britain
Economy: Tourism

Montserrat has been British since 1632. Since
1960 it has been a United Kingdom Overseas Territory with self-government. It has a parliament,
governor and chief of the government. The flag
is dark blue with the Union Jack in the union. The
arms to the right show a shield in a white circle,
with a woman holding a cross in her right hand
and a harp in her left. It recalls the Irish immi-
grants of 1632.

Native name: Montserrat
German: Montserrat
French: Montserrat
Spanish: Montserrat

AMERICA

Nicaragua

Native name: Nicaragua
German: Nicaragua
French: Nicaragua

Republic of Nicaragua

Capital: Managua
Area:120,254 sq. km.
Population: 5,480,000
Language: Spanish
Currency: Co/rdoba

Member: OAS, UN
Economy: Fruit, meat,
coffee, sugar, gold

The flag scarcely differs from that of the Central American Federation, which existed from 1821 to 1838. The two blue stripes symbolize the Caribbean Sea and Pacific Ocean, which border Nicaragua. The white stripe stands for peace in the country. The triangular coat of arms on the white stripe stands for equality, the Phyrgian cap for freedom, and the five volcanoes represent the five former states of the Federation.

Netherlands Antilles

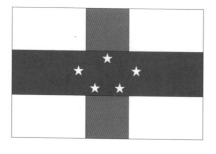

Native name: Nederlandse Antillen
    (Dutch)
German: Niederländische Antillen
French: Altilles néerlandaises
Spanish: Antillas Neerlandesas

Netherlands Antilles

Capital: Willemstad
Area: 800 sq. km.
Population: 180,592
Languages: Dutch,
Papiamento, English,
Spanish

Currency: Antillean Guilder
Belongs to: Netherlands
Economy: Petroleum products are exported

The Netherlands Antilles consists of five islands: Curaçao is the largest, the others are Bonaire, Saint Maarten (southern part), Saint Eustatius, and Saba. The Antilles have belonged to the Netherlands since 1630 and attained autonomy in 1954. The islands all have their own flags; only Sint Eustatius uses the national flag. White, blue and red are the colors of the Netherlands. The five stars on the blue stripe represent the five islands.

Panama

Republic of Panama

Capital: Panama
Area: 406,752 sq. km.
Population: 2,984,000
Language: Spanish
Currency: Balboa, US
Dollar

Member: OAS, UN
Economy: Fish, shrimp,
bananas, pineapple,
melons

The colors of the flag are based on those of the country's leading political parties: The Liberals use red, the Conservatives blue; white stands for the peaceful co-existence of the parties. The two stars symbolize the cities of Panama and Colón, the blue also stands for purity, the red for law and order.

Native name: Panamá
German: Panama
French: Panama

Paraguay

Republic of Paraguay

Capital: Asunción
Area: 406,752 sq. km.
Population: 5,643,000
Languages: Spanish,
Guarani
Currency: Guarani

Member: OAS, UN
Economy: Fruits for oils,
animal fats and oils

Paraguay's flag has an unusual feature, having different emblems on the front and back. Beyond that, the blue stands for good-heartedness, the white for peace and unity, and the red for courage, equality and justice. The star in the coat of arms on the front is a symbol of independence. On the back is the seal of the Treasury Department.

Native name: Paraguay (Spanish)
German: Paraguay
French: Paraguay

Peru

Native name: Perú (Spanish)
German: Peru
French: Pérou

Republic of Peru

Capital: Lima
Area: 1,285,216 sq. km.
Population: 27,148,000
Languages: Spanish,
Quechua, Almara
Currency: New Sol

Member: OAS, UN
Economy: Mining, fish,
clothing

The wide red stripes stand for the blood shed by patriots. The white central stripe symbolizes law and justice. Red was also the color of the Inca kings' tassels, and white was the royal color. The arms show a shield with symbols of the country's animal and plant life. The flag was introduced in 1825.

Puerto Rico

Native name: Puerto Rico (English & Spanish)
French: Porto Rico

Commonwealth of Puerto Rico

Capital: San Juan
Area: 8,959 sq. km.
Population: 3,900,000
Languages: English, Spanish Currency: US Dollar

Belongs to: USA
Economy: Rum and drink concentrates, clothing and electronic products are exported

Puerto Rico was ceded to the USA in 1898, after the Spanish-American War. In 1917 the Population received US citizenship. Puerto Rico is now a commonwealth, meaning that it is extensively autonomous, as are the states, but the Population may not vote in the USA. The flag resembles that of Cuba except that the stripes are red instead of blue, and the triangle is blue instead of red.

St. Kitts and Nevis

Federation of St. Kitts and Nevis

Capital: Basseterre
Area: 269 sq. km.
Population: 46,700
Language: English
Currency: East Caribbean Dollar

Member: CARICOM, OAS, UN
Economy: Machines and transport equipment, sugar and products

The green triangle symbolizes the fruitful soil of the land. The black stripe stands for the African heritage of the Population, most of whom are descended from African slaves. The red triangle recalls the islands' troubled past, including slavery and colonial rule. Independence was finally attained in 1983. The stars represent the two islands; the thin yellow stripes stand for the sun.

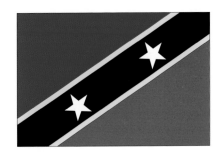

Native name: St. Kitts and Nevis
German: St. Kitts und Nevis
French: Saint-Christophe-et-Niévès;
        Saint-Christophe-et-Nevis
Spanish: San Cristo/bal y Nieves

St. Lucia

St. Lucia

Capital: Castries
Area: 613.3 sq. km.
Population: 161,000
Language: English
Currency: East Caribbean Dollar

Member: CARICOM ,OAS, UN
Economy: Bananas, beer, clothing

The blue background stands for both the sky and the ocean. The triangle symbolizes the island; yellow stands for sunshine and well-being, black for the mainly black population, and the white stripe for the white population. The flag exists in this form since 1979. It was designed by a native artist.

Native name: Saint Lucia
German: Saint Lucia
French: Sainte-Lucie
Spanish: Santa Lucía

St. Vincent and the Grenadines

Native name: Saint Vincent and the
Grenadines
German: St. Vincent und Grenadinen
French: Saint-Vincent-et-les-Grena-
dines

St. Vincent and the Grenadines

Capital: Kingstown
Area: 389,3 sq. km.
Population: 109,000
Language: English
Currency: East Caribbean
Dollar

Member: CARICOM, OAS,
UN
Economy: Bananas,
flour, rice

The blue stripe at left stands for the Caribbean
Sea and cloudless sky, yellow symbolizes the
warmth and happiness of the people as well as
the sandy beaches, green stands for the luxuriant
vegetation of the islands and the energy of the
people. The stylized diamonds stand for "V for
victory" and the name of the main island.

Suriname

Native name: Suriname
German: Suriname
French: Suriname
Spanish: Surinam

Republic of Suriname

Capital: Paramaribo
Area: 163,265 sq. km.
Population: 438,000
Language: Dutch
Currency: Suriname Dol-
lar

Member: CARICOM, OAS,
UN
Economy: Aluminum,
fish and sea creatures

The green stripes symbolize the fruitfulness of
the land and the hope seen by the Population in
their independence from the Netherlands, attained in 1975. White stands for peace, freedom
and justice. Red symbolizes love for the land and
progress. The golden star stands for unity and the
country's golden future. The colors of the political
parties are also represented in red and green.

Trinidad and Tobago

Republic of Trinidad and Tobago

Capital: Port of Spain
Area: 5,128 sq. km.
Population: 1,313,000
Language: English
Currency: Trinidad-and-Tobago Dollar

Member: CARICOM, OAS, UN
Economy: Fuels,lubricants, chemical products

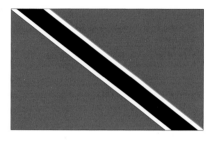

Trinidad and Tobago became independent in 1962, and the flag has been unchanged since then. The red color represents the strength of the people, the black diagonal stripe is the unifying power embodying the people's solidarity, and also represents the natural resources of petroleum and natural gas. The white lines stand for the sea that links the two main islands, and for the equality of all peoples.

Native name: Trinidad and Tobago
German: Trinidad und Tobago
French: Trinite'-et-Tobago, Trinidad-et-Tobago
Spanish: Trinidad y Tobago

Turks and Caicos Islands

Turks and Caicos Islands

Capital: Cockburn Town
Area: 430 sq. km.
Population: 20,014
Languages: English, Creole
Currency: US Dollar

Belongs to: Great Britain
Economy: Main exports are aquatic fruits

The Turks and Caicos Islands consist of more than 30 islands, eight of which are inhabited. The population consists of Blacks and Mullatos. The status since 1962 is that of a United Kingdom Overseas Territory, with self-government. The flag has a dark blue ground with the Union Jack in the union and the arms of the Turks and Caicos Islands to the right, consisting of a yellow shield with a lobster, a snail and a cactus.

Native name: Turks and Caicos Islands (English)
German: Turks- und Caicos-Inseln
French: Iles Turks-et-Caicos
Spanish: Islas Turcas y Caicos

Uruguay

Republic of Uruguay

Capital: Montevideo
Area: 176,215 sq. km.
Population: 3,380,000
Language: Spanish
Currency: Uruguayan
Peso

Member: OAS, UN
Economy: deep-frozen
products, leather goods,
grains

Native name: Uruguay
German: Uruguay
French" Uruguay

The colors of the flag correspond to those of the
Argentine flag, while the form itself comes from
the American flag. The nine stripes represent the
nine original provinces of the land. Blue stands
for peace, white for freedom. The sun, also called
"Sol de Mayo" (Sun of Freedom), has been the
national emblem since 1815 and symbolizes its
independence.

Venezuela

Bolivarian Republic of Venezuela

Capital: Caracas
Area: 912,050 sq. km.
Population: 25,674,000
Language: Spanish
Currency: Bolivar

Member: CARICOM
(observer), OAS, UN
Economy: Mining, metal
and chemical products

Native name: Venezuela
German: Venezuela
French: Venezuela

The colors of gold, blue and red are still interpre-
ted as in the freedom movement of 1806, when
the flag was first flown in this color combination.
The golden South America is separated by the
blue sea from blood-red Spain. Blue also stands
for freedom, red for courage and gold for the
original federation. The seven stars represent the
seven provinces of the country.

United States

United States of America

Capital: Washington
Area: 9,809,155 sq. km.
Population: 290,810,000
Languages: English, Spanish
Currency: US Dollar

Member: G-8, NAFTA, NATO, OAS, OECD, OSZE, UN
Economy: Computers, machines, vehicles and parts, chemical products

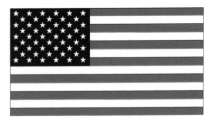

Since 1818 the number of stars in the upper left corner of the flag has equaled the number of states of the USA. The last change took place in 1960 when Hawaii became a state; since then there have been 50 stars. The 13 stripes refer to the founding colonies that federated to form the United States and declared their independence from Great Britain. The white color also stands for purity and red for bravery.

Native name: United States (English)
German: Vereinigte Staaten
French: États-Unis
Spanish: Estados Unidos

Alabama
The Yellowhammer State
Area: 135,775 sq. km.
Capital: Montgomery

Alaska
The Last Frontier
Area: 1,700,138 sq. km.
Capital: Juneau

Arizona
The Apache State
Area: 295,276 sq. km.
Capital: Phoenix

Arkansas
The Natural State
Area: 137,742 sq. km.
Capital: Little Rock

Kalifornien
The Golden State
Area: 424,002 sq. km.
Capital: Sacramento

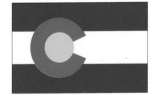

Colorado
The Centennial State
Area: 269,618 sq. km.
Capital: Denver

AMERICA

Connecticut
The Constitution State
Area: 14,358 sq. km.
Capital: Hartford

Delaware
The First State
Area: 6,448 sq. km.
Capital: Dover

Florida
The Sunshine State
Area: 170,314 sq. km.
Capital: Tallahassee

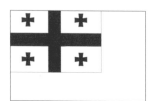

Georgia *wrong Georgia!*
The Peach State
Area: 153,952 sq. km.
Capital: Atlanta

Hawaii
The Aloha State
Area: 28,313 sq. km.
Capital: Honolulu

Idaho
The Gem State
Area: 216 456 km²
Capital: Boise City

Illinois
The Prairie State
Area: 150,007 sq. km.
Capital: Springfield

Indiana
The Hoosier State
Area: 94,328 sq. km.
Capital: Indianapolis

Iowa
The Hawkeye State
Area: 145 754 km²
Capital: Des Moines

Kansas
The Sunflower State
Area: 213,111 sq. km.
Capital: Topeka

Kentucky
The Bluegrass State
Area: 104,665 sq. km.
Capital: Frankfort

Louisiana
The Pelican State
Area: 134,275 sq. km.
Capital: Baton Rouge

AMERICA and the States

Maine
The Pine Tree State
Area: 91 653 km²
Capital: Augusta

Maryland
The Old Line State
Area: 32 134 km²
Capital: Annapolis

Massachusetts
The Bay State
Area: 27 337 km²
Capital: Boston

Michigan
The Wolverine State
Area: 250 465 km²
Capital: Lansing

Minnesota
The North Star State
Area: 225 182 km²
Capital: Saint Paul

Mississippi
The Magnolia State
Area: 125 443 km²
Capital: Jackson

Missouri
The Show Me State
Area: 180 546 km²
Capital: Jefferson City

Montana
The Treasure State
Area: 380 850 km²
Capital: Helena

Nebraska
The Cornhusker State
Area: 200 358 km²
Capital: Lincoln

Nevada
The Silver State
Area: 286 367 km²
Capital: Carson City

New Hampshire
The Granite State
Area: 24 219 km²
Capital: Concord

New Jersey
The Garden State
Area: 22 590 km²
Capital: Trenton

AMERICA

New Mexico
The Cactus State
Area: 314 939 km²
Capital: Santa Fé

New York
The Empire State
Area: 141 080 km²
Capital: Albany

North Carolina
The Tar Heel State
Area: 139 397 km²
Capital: Raleigh

North Dakota
The Sioux State
Area: 183 123 km²
Capital: Bismarck

Ohio
The Buckeye State
Area: 116 103 km²
Capital: Columbus

Oklahoma
The Sooner State
Area: 181 048 km²
Capital: Oklahoma City

Oregon
The Beaver State
Area: 254 819 km²
Capital: Salem

Pennsylvania
The Keystone State
Area: 119 291 km²
Capital: Harrisburg

Rhode Island
Little Rhody
Area: 4 002 km²
Capital: Providence

South Carolina
The Palmetto State
Area: 82 902 km²
Capital: Columbia

South Dakota
The Mount Rushmore State
Area: 199 744 km²
Capital: Pierre

Tennessee
Volunteer State
Area: 109 158 km²
Capital: Nashville

Texas
The Lone Star State
Area: 695 676 km²
Capital: Austin

Utah
The Beehive State
Area: 219 902 km²
Capital: Salt Lake City

Vermont
The Green Mountain State
Area: 24 903 km²
Capital: Montpelier

Virginia
Old Dominion
Area: 110 792 km²
Capital: Richmond

Washington
The Evergreen State
Area: 184 672 km²
Capital: Olympia

West Virginia
The Mountain State
Area: 62 759 km²
Capital: Charleston

Wisconsin
The Badger State
Area: 169 643 km²
Capital: Madison

Wyoming
The Equality State
Area: 253 349 km²
Capital: Cheyenne

Virgin Islands

American
Virgin Islands

Capital: Charlotte Amalie
Area: 352 sq. km.
Population: 125,000

Languages: English, Spanish, Creole
Currency: US Dollar
Economy: Tourism

The official status of the Virgin Islands is that of an unincorporated territory of the USA. The islands previously belonged to the British, then the Danes. The flag much resembles that of the US Army, with a yellow eagle with outspread wings on a white ground. It holds an olive branch and three arrows in its claws. The initials are those of the Virgin Islands.

TURKEY

GEORGIA

ARMENIA AZERBAIJAN

KAZAKHSTAN

MONGOLIA

LEBANON
ISRAEL
IRAN
SYRIA
UZBEKISTAN
PALESTINIAN
TERRITORIES JORDAN
IRAQ
TURKMENISTAN

KYRGYZSTAN

IRAN
TAJIKISTAN

CHINA

SAUDI ARABIA
AFGHANISTAN

QATAR
PAKISTAN

UNITED ARAB
EMIRATES
NEPAL
BHUTAN

OMAN
INDIA
BANGLADESH

YEMEN
MYANMAR

LAOS

THAILAND

VIETNAM

CAMBODIA

SRI LANKA

MALDIVES

MALAYSIA

SINGAPORE

Asia is the largest continent and contains almost 30% of the earth's land surface. If one adds its islands and inland seas, Asia has an area of 44.2 million square kilometers. Over 3.5 billion people, more than half the world's population, live in Asia. Asia borders on Europe on the west, and the boundary has been defined variously. Sometimes one finds Turkey, Georgia, Armenia and Azerbaijan ranked as belonging to Europe. In this book they are in the Asian chapter.

One must basically divide this huge continent into Asia Minor, Central, Northern, Eastern, Southern and Southeast Asia. In all, the continent consists of 46 independent countries recognized by the UN. Many Near Eastern and Persian Gulf countries express their belonging to the Arabic peoples through the pan-Arabic flag colors of red, white and black, while the color green stands for Islam. In Eastern and Southeast Asia Buddhism and Christianity are more strongly represented. Many countries in Southeast Asia were colonized by France and Britain. Only in 1977 was the last British flag lowered, and the island state of Hong Kong is now a specially administered region with its own flag.

JAPAN

TH
A

IWAN

PHILIPPINES

EI

EAST TIMOR

ASIA

ASIA
Afghanistan

Islamic Republic of Afghanistan

Native name: Afghanistan (Pashtu),
  Afgha/nestân (Dari)
German: Afghanistan
French: Afghanistan
Spanish: Afghanistán

Capital: Kabul
Area: 652,225 sq. km.
Population: 28,766,000
Languages: Pashtu, Dari
Currency: Afghani

Member: UN
Economy: foods and
fruits

Because of its changing history, Afghanistan has had over 20 different flags in the last hundred years. The present flag goes back to the kingdom of 1931 and is used again since the fall of the Taliban. Black stands for the dark past, red for the fight for independence, and green for the attainment of independence. The arms symbolize Islam.

Armenia

Republic of Armenien

Native name: Hayastan
German: Armenien
French: Arménie
Spanish: Armenia

Capital: Eriwan
Area: 29,743 sq. km.
Population: 3,056,000
Language: Armenian
Currency: Dram

Member: GUS, OSZE, UN
Economy: Precious and
semi-precious stones,
metals

The red stripe recalls the long bloody fight for Armenian independence from their Turkish over-lords. The blue stripe symbolizes the wide sky over the land and the character of the people, the orange stripe stands for the people's courage and strength. The flag became the state flag after independence from the Soviet Union in 1991.

Azerbaijan

Republic of Azerbaijan

Capital: Baku
Area: 86,600 sq. km.
Population: 8,233,000
Language: Azerbaijani
Currency: Azerbaijan
Manat

Member: UUS, OSZE, UN
Economy: Energy
carriers, foods, pleasure
goods

The blue stripe symbolizes the sky over the land, but also the Azer people. Ted stands for freedom and green for the fruitful land. The crescent moon and star (and the color green) are symbols of Islam. The eight points on the star stand for the eight peoples of the country. The flag was reintroduced after the collapse of the Soviet Union in 1991.

Native name: Azärbaycan
German: Aserbaidschan
French: Azerbaídjan
Spanish: Azerbaiyán

Bahrain

Kingdom of Bahrain

Capital: Manama
Area: 715.9 sq. km.
Population: 712,000
Language: Arabic
Currency: Bahrain-Dinar

Member: UN
Economy: Petroleum

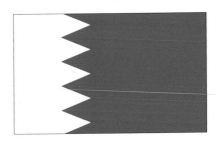

The dominant color of red was originally the color Bahraini Moslems. The white stripe, originally not pointed, was introduced in 1820 as suggested by the British. Until then the flag had been plain red. Since 2002 the line has been defined as having five points, representing the five pillars of Islam.

Native name: Al-Bahrayn
German: Bahrain
French: Bahrein
Spanish: Bahráin

ASIA

Bangladesh

People's Republic of Bangladesh

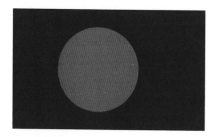

Capital: Dhaka
Area: 147,570 sq. km.
Population: 138,066,000
Language: Bengali
Currency: Taka

Member: UN
Economy:
Clothing,knitted goods,
hosiery

Native name: Bangladesh
German: Bangladesch
French: Basngladesh
Spanish: Bangladesh

The green main color of the flag stands for the fruitful land, but also for the Islamic faith to which the majority of the people belong. The red circle symbolizes the bloody battle for independence against the British colonial power in the 1930s. Originally the outlines of the country were shown in yellow in the circle.

Bhutan

Kingdom of Bhutan

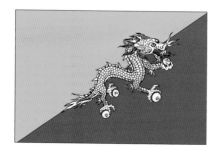

Capital: Thimphu
Area: 38,394 sq. km.
Population: 874,000
Language: Dzongkha
Currency: Ngultrum

Member: UN
Economy: power, wood,
calcium carbide

Native name: Druk Yul
German: Bhutan
French: Bhoutan
Spanish: Bután

The left saffron-yellow triangle stands for the secular and religious authority of the king. The red triangle is dedicated to Buddhism. The dragon stands for the name of the country, "Dragon Realm", in Tibetan "Druk yul". The white color of the dragon symbolizes the loyalty of the various peoples and their honesty. The jewels held in the dragon's claws symbolize well-being and perfection.

Brunei Darussalam

Brunei Darussalam

Capital: Bandar Seri Begawan Area: 5,765 sq. km.
Population: 356,000
Language: Malayan
Currency: Brunei-Dollar

Member: ASEAN, UN
Economy: Petroleum, and oil products, finished goods

In 1906 three governors signed a treaty with the British government to regulate the mutual rights and duties: the sultan, whose color is yellow, and two viziers, whose colors were white and black. The country's first flag was composed of these three colors. In 1959 the red emblem of state was added, symbolizing justice, peace and Islam.

Native name: Brunei Darussalam
German: Brunei Darussalam
French: Brunei
Spanish: Brunei

Kingdom of Cambodia

Cambodia

Capital: Phnom Penh
Area: 181,135 sq. km.
Population: 13,404,000
Language: Khmer
Currency: Riel

Member: ASEAN, UN
Economy: Textiles and clothing, rubber and wood

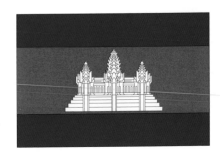

Blue is the color of the king, red that of the Khmer people. The central symbol shows a stylized temple of Angkor Wat, which refers to the glorious past and tradition of the country. The white color of the temple stands for belief in the king. The flag was introduced in 1993.

Native name: Kâmpuchea
German: Kambodscha
French: Cambodge
Spanish: Camboya

ASIA

China

Native name: Zhonggue
German: China
French: Chine
Spanish: China

People's Republic of China

Capital: Peking (Beijing)
Area: 9,572,419 sq. km.
Population:
1,295,660,000
Language: Chinese
Currency: Renmibni Yuan

Member: UN
Economy: Textiles, office machines, information and electronic techno-logy

Red is both the color of communism and the tra-ditional color of China and the Han Chinese. The large star stands for the Communist Party, while the four small ones represent the four classes of the people: workers, farmers, bourgeois and patriotic capitalists. The flag was introduced in this form in 1949.

Georgia

Native name: Sak'art'velo
German: Georgien
French: Géorgie
Spanish: Georgia

Georgia

Capital: Tiflis
Area: 69,700 sq. km.
Population: 5,126,000
Language: Georgian
Currency: Lari

Member: GUS, OSZE, UN
Economy: Wine, sugar,copper, gold, scrap metal

The flag with the five crosses stems from the Middle Ages, when it was the flag of the Geor-gian kings. As of 1921 Georgia used a variant of the Soviet flag; in 199 a black-red-white flag was introduced, but after a people's revolution in 2004 it was abolished. The present flag symbolizes the widespread Georgian Orthodox faith of the popu-lation.

India

Republic of India

Capital: New Delhi
Area: 3,287,263 sq. km.
Population:
1,064,399,000
Languages: Hindi, English, National languages

Currency: Indian Rupee
Member: UN
Economy: Jewels and
jewelry, textiles, clothing

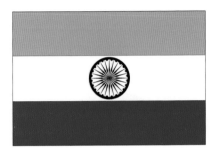

The saffron yellow stripe incorporates the people's courage and sacrifice and is also the color of the Hindus and Sikhs. White stands for peace and truth, green for faith in general and Islam. The sun disc in the center is blue and embodies the sky; its white rays symbolize the sun, without which life would not be possible.

Native name: Bhurat Ganarujya
(Hindi)
German: Indien
French: Inde
Spanish India (la)

Indonesia

Republic of Indonesia

Capital: Jakarta
Area: 1,912,988 sq. km.
Population: 214,674,000
Language: Indonesian
Currency: Rupiah

Member: ASEAN, OPEC,
UN
Economy: fuels,
oils, machines, foods

The red and white colors were already used in the 13th century and now serve as the national colors. Red embodies physical life, white stands for spiritual life. Together they stand for the unity of human life in its duality of body and spirit. The flag was adopted in 1945, when the country declared its independence, which it actually attained only in 1949.

Native name: Indonesia
German: Indonesien
French: Indonésie
Spanish: Indonesia

ASIA

Iran

Native name: Îrân
German: Iran
French: Iran
Spanish: Irán

Islamic Republic of Iran

Capital: Teheran
Area: 1,648,000 sq. km.
Population: 66,392,000
Language: Persian
Currency: Rial

Member: OPEC, UN
Economy: Petroleum
makes up 80% of the
exports

The colors of green, white and red are the traditional colors of the country, symbolizing Islam, peace and bravery. The arms in the center consist of four half-moons grouped around a sword. These five elements embody the five basic principles of Islam. The stylized lettering at the edges of the white stripe say "Allah is great" 22 times.

Iraq   Republic of Iraq

Native name: Al Iraq
German: Irak
French: Iraq
Spanish: Iraq

Capital: Bagdad
Area: 438,317 sq. km.
Population: 24,700,000
Language: Arabic
Currency: Iraqi Dinar

Member: OPEC, UN
Economy: crude
oil, agriculture, grains,
vegetables, dates

The flag of Iraq consists of the pan-Arabic colors, with red standing for courage in battle, white for dignity and black for the victory of Islam. The green color of the stars also indicates Islam and the prophet Mohammed. The three stars stand for Egypt, Iraq and Syria, which tried in 1963 to create a United Arab Republic, which did not succeed.

Israel

State of Israel

Capital: Jerusalem
Area: 20,991 sq. km.
Population: 6,688,000
Languages: Hebrew,
Arabic
Currency: New Shekel

Member: UN
Economy: Building mate-
rials, ceramics, glass,
machines, vehicles

The white field represents the purity of Zionistic ideals. Blue stands for the sky. These two colors and the stripe pattern come from the Jewish prayer shawl. In the center of the white field is the Star of David, a Jewish symbol since the Middle Ages. The flag was introduced as the national flag in 1948.

Native name: Yisra'el (Hebrew)
German: Israel
French: Israël
Spanish: Israel

Japan

Japan

Capital: Tokyo
Area: 377,837 sq. km.
Population: 127,573,000
Language: Japanese
Currency: Yen

Member: G-8, OECD, UN
Economy: vehicles and
parts, machines, electro-
technology

The white ground of the flag symbolizes the sky and the purity of the nation. The red sun disc stands for peace and prosperity. The red color symbolizes righteousness and clear understanding in Japan. The sun is an ancient symbol in Japan, whose former emperors saw themselves as direct descendants of the sun god.

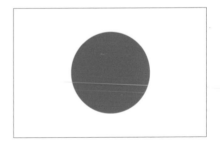

Native name: Nihon, Nippon
German: Japan
French: Japon
Spanish: Japón

ASIA

Jordan

Hashemite Kingdom of Jordan

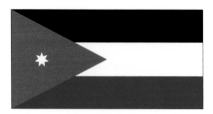

Capital: Amman Area: 89,342 sq. km. Population: 5,308,000 Language: Arabic Currency: Jordanian Dinar

Member: UN Economy: Clothing, chemical products, raw materials

Native name: Al-Urdun
German: Jordanien
French: Jordanie
Spanish: Jordania

Each color represents one of the country's families of caliphs: Black stands for the Abbasids, white for the Omajjads, green for the Fatimids and for Mohammed, and red for the Hashemites, from whom the modern kings are presumably descended. The white star incorporates the first seven verses of the Koran.

Kazachstan

Republic of Kazakhstan

Capital: Astana Area: 2,717,300 sq. km. Population: Kazakh , Currency: Tenge

Member: GUS, OSZE, UN Economy: petroleum, natural gas, metals, foods

Native name: Qazaqstan Respublikasy
German: Kasachstan
French: Kazakhstan
Spanish: Kazajistán

Blue stands for the Kazakh people, for peace and plenty, and for the endless sky that spreads over the great land. The sun and the eagle under it express the Kazakh people's love for freedom and their ideals. The yellow design refers to the renowned ornamental art used in making carpets. The flag was introduced in 1992.

Korea (North)

Democratic People's Republic of Korea, or North Korea

Capital: Pyongyang
Area: 122,762 sq. km.
Population: 22,612,000
Language: Korean
Currency: Won

Member: UN
Economy: foods, live animals, textiles

Red stands for the communist revolution, blue for the sovereignty of the state, and white for the unity of the people, plus for purity, strength and worth. Blue also symbolizes the Sea of Japan and Yellow Sea, which enclose Korea on both sides. Until 1948 North and South Korea had the same flag.

Native name: Choson
German: Nordkorea
France: Corée du Nord
Spanish: Corel del Norte

Korea (South)

Republic of Korea, or South Korea

Capital: Seoul
Area: 99,313 sq. km.
Population: 47,912,000
Language: Korean
Currency: Won

Member: OECD, UN
Economy: Information technology, radio, TV, vehicles

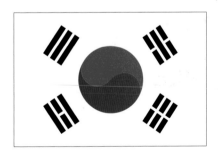

White stands for peace. In the center of the flag is the ying-yang sombol, standing for the self-completing opposites of the country (life and death, man and woman, day and night). The four groups of lines (trigrams) symbolize the elements: water, earth, fire and sky, as well as the four seasons and four directions.

Native name: Han'guk
German: Südkorea
French: Corée du Sud
Spanish: Corea del Sur

ASIA

Kuwait

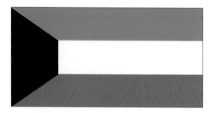

State of Kuwait

Capital: Kuwait
Area: 17,818 sq. km.
Population: 2,396,000
Language: Arabic
Currency: Kuwaiti Dinar

Member: OPEC, UN
Economy: petroleum and
its products make up
92% of the exports.

Native name: Al-Kuwait
German: Kuwait
French: Koweït
Spanish: Kuwait

The flag of Kuwait consists of the pan-Arabic colors. Black stands for the battles of the past, green for the fruitful meadows of the country, white for the purity of past and present deeds, and red for the great future prospects of the Arabic peoples. The flag was introduced in 1961.

Kyrgyzstan

Kyrgyz Republic

Capital: Bishkek
Area: 199,900 sq. km.
Population: 5,052,000
Languages: Kyrgyz, Russian
Currency: Kyrgyz-Som

Member: GUS, OSZE, UN
Economy: precious
metals, mineral products, textiles, leather

Native name: Kyrgyz Respublikasy
(Kyrgyz)
German: Kirgisistan
French: Kirghizistan, le Kirghizstan
Spanish: Kirguizistán

The red color honors national hero Manas, who is said to have united the 40 Kyrgyz tribes under a red banner; the 40-rayed sun in the center of the flag also refers to this. Within the sun there is the roof of a yurt, the typical Kyrgyz nomads' tent. Until 1992 Kyrgyzstan was a Soviet republic; since 1992 the country is independent and flies this flag.

Laos

Democratic People's Republic of Laos

Capital: Vientiane
Area: 236,000 sq. km.
Population: 5,660,000
Language: Laotian
Currency: Kip

Member: ASEAN, UN
Economy:
Clothing, electricity, wood
and wood products

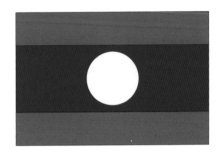

The red border stripes represent the heart and blood of the Laotian people. Blue symbolizes prosperity and a glowing future for the country. The white circle stands for the moon, which is said to bring luck. Laos was a French colony until 1953. The flag was introduced in 1975 when the country became a democratic people's republic.

Native name: Sathalanalat Paxathipa-
tai Paxaxon Lao
German: Laos
French: Laos
Spanish: Laos

Lebanon

Lebanese Republic

Capital: Beirut
Area: 10,452 sq. km.
Population: 4,498,000
Language: Arabic
Currency: Lebanese
Pound

Member: UN
Economy: Jewelry, foods,
metals

The red stripes stand for the people's self-sacrifice, white symbolizes peace. The tree in the center is a cedar, a symbol of holiness and eternity since ancient times. In the bible, the cedar was already linked with Lebanon. The flag was introduced in its present form on Lebanon's independence in 1943.

Native name: Al-Lubnan
German: Libanon
French: Liban
Spanish: Líbano

ASIA

Malaysia

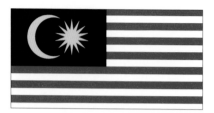

Malaysia

Capital: Kuala Lumpur
Area: 329,733 sq. km.
Population: 24,774,000
Language: Malay
Currency: Ringit

Member: ASEAN, UN
Economy: Electronic components, electric machines, petroleum

Native name: Malaysia
German: Malaysia
French: Malaisie
Spanish: Malasia

The Malaysian flag was inspired by the US flag; the colors are also those of the former colonial power, Great Britain. Red and white are also traditional colors of the country. The blue union stands for the unity of the people, the star and crescent moon are symbols of Islam. The 14 stripes stand for the 13 states and the central government.

Maldives

Republic of Malediven

Capital: Male
Area: 298 sq. km.
Population: 293,000
Language: Divehi
Currency: Rufiyaa

Member: UN
Economy: fish and fish products, clothing

Native name: Dhivehi Raajje
German: Malediven
French: Maldives
Spanish: Maldivas

Red has been the flag color of the seafaring people of the Maldives since the 19th century. Today it stands for the blood shed by national heroes who fought for independence. The green stands for Islam, and for freedom and progress. The crescent moon is also a symbol of Islam, the faith of the majority of the people.

Mongolia

Mongolia

Capital: Ulan Bator
Area: 1,564,100 sq. km.
Population: 2,480,000
Language: Mongolian
Currency: Tugrik

Member: UN
Economy: Copper, textiles, precious metals

Red, blue and yellow are the traditional Mongol colors. Red symbolizes the people's joy of life, blue the sky and eternity, and yellow unending friendship. The symbol on the hoist is called Soyombo and is an old symbol of peace and independence. From 1945 to 1992 the flag also bore the yellow star of Communism.

Native name: Mongol Uls
German: Mongolei
French: Mongolie
Spanish: Mongolia

Union Myanmar, or Burma

Myanmar

Capital: Rangoon
Area: 676,552sq. km.
Population: 49,363,000
Language: Burmese
Currency: Kyat

Member: ASEAN, UN
Economy: natural gas, agricultural and forest products

Red stands for the courage and tenacity of the people, the blue rectangle in the union for the night sky that radiates rest and peace. White stands for purity. The 14 white stars in the blue union stand for the country's 14 provinces, the gear wheel for industry, and the rice ear for agriculture. The flag was introduced in 1974.

Native name: Myanma Naigngan
German: Myanmar
French: Birmanie, le Myanmar
Spanish: Birmania, Myanmar

ASIA

Nepal

Native name: Nepal
German: Nepal
French: Népal
Spanish: Nepal

Kingdom of Nepal

Capital: Katmandu
Area: 147,181 sq. km.
Population: 24,660,000
Language: Nepalese
Currency: Nepalese Rupee

Member: UN
Economy: Carpets, texti-
les, clothing, skins and
hides.

The Nepalese flag is the only national flag that is not square or rectangular. The shape with its two summits refers to the country's situation in the mountains. Red is the color of Nepal and its national flower, the rhododendron. The blue edge stands for peace. The star and crescent in the upper half stand for the royal house, the sun in the lower part for the Rana dynasty. The two parts symbolize the main religions.

Oman

Native name: Uman
German: Oman
French: Oman
Spanish: Omán

Sultanate Oman

Capital: Muscat
Area: 309,500 sq. km.
Population: 2,599,000
Language: Arabic
Currency: Rial Omani

Member: UN
Economy: Petroleum and
natural gas, (80% of
exports)

Red is the color of the Charidjite Moslems, white symbolizes peace and stands for the Imam, the country's religious leader. Green represents the fruitful areas and the "green mountain". The state emblem at the upper left shows two short swords crossed on a belt and an Arab dagger. The flag was last changed in 1975.

Pakistan

Islamic Republic of Pakistan

Capital: Islamabad
Area: 796,095 sq. km.
Population: 148,439,000
Language: Urdu
Currency: Pakistani
Rupee

Member: UN
Economy: textiles, knit-
ted goods, bed linens,
clothing

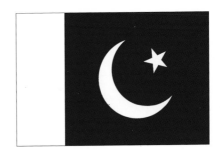

Both the green color and the star and crescent moon are symbols of Islam, the dominant religion in Pakistan. The half-moon also stands for progress and the star for knowledge. The white stripe at the hoist represents the religious minorities in the country, particularly Hindus. The flag was introduced in 1947 when Pakistan was founded.

Native name: Pakistan
German: Pakistan
French: Pakistan
Spanish: Pakistán

Palestinian Territories

Palestinian Territories

Capital: Ramallah
Area: 6020 sq. km.
Population: 3,367,000
Languages: Arabic,
Hebrew, English
Currency: Israeli Shekel,
Jordanian Dinar

Economy: Services lead
with 88% of the econo-
my; exporting is mainly
to Israel.

The Palestinian territories have been partially autonomous since 1994; since 2002 they have had their own constitution. They are recognized as a state by only 92 countries. Since the death of PLO leader Yassir Arafat there is again hope of settling the eternal conflict and coming closer to peace. The flag shows the pan-Arabic colors, green for Islam, red for sacrifice in battle, black for mourning and white for memory.

Native name: As-Sulta Al-Wataniyya
(Arabic)
German: Palästinensische Gebiete
French: Autorité palestinienne
Spanish: Autoridad Palestina

ASIA

Philippines

Republic of the Philippines

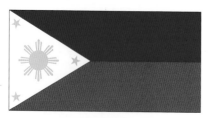

Native name: Pilipinas
German: Philippinen
French: Philippines
Spanish: Filipinas

Capital: Manila
Area: 300,000 sq. km.
Population: 81,503,000
Language: Filipino
Currency: Philippine Peso

Member: ASEAN, UN
Economy: electronics,
electrotechnology, clo-
thing, machines

The blue stripe embodies patriotism and idealism,
the red stands for bravery. The white triangle
symbolizes purity and peace. The three small
stars represent the three main regions of the
country: Luzon, the Visayan Archipelago and
Mindanao. The sun in the triangle stands with
its eight rays for the eight provinces that initially
opposed Spain.

Qatar

State of Qatar

Native name: Qatar
German: Katar
French: Qatar
Spanish: Qatar

Capital: Doha
Area: 11,437 sq. km.
Population: 624,000
Language: Arabic
Currency: Qatar Rial

Member: OPEC, UN
Economy: Petroleum,
fertilizers

Red and white are the traditional colors of the
sheikdoms on the Persian Gulf. But the strong
rays of the sun makes red cloth darken quickly,
and the originally red color was changed to a
brownish shade. The flag also differs thus from
the flag of Bahrain. Today the number of points
has been fixed at

Saudi Arabia

Kingdom of Saudi-Arabia

Capital: Riyadh
Area: 2,240,000 sq. km.
Population: 22,528,000
Language: Arabic
Currency: Saudi Riyal

Member: OPEC, UN
Economy: Petroleum and
its products, petroche-
micals

Green is the color of Islam and the prophet
Mohammed. The sword symbolizes battle and
the fighters' obligation to protect the holy cities of
Islam, Mecca and Medina. The writing is the Islamic statement of faith: "There is no god but Allah
and Mohammed is his prophet."

Native name: Al Arabiyah as-Saudiyah
German: Saudi-Arabien
French: Arabie saoudite
Spanish: Arabia Saudi

Singapore

Republic of Singapore

Capital: Singapore
Area: 682.7 sq. km.
Population: 4,250,000
Languages: Malay, Tamil,
Chinese, English Curren-
cy: Singapore Dollar

Member: ASEAN, UN
Economy: Fuels, office
machines, chemical pro-
ducts

The red stripe stands for equality and brotherhood; the white stripe symbolizes the purity of
the human spirit and eternal loyalty. The half-
moon symbolizes the young nation at the beginning of its rise. The five stars symbolize the five
ideals that are to be attained: Democracy, peace,
progress, justice and equality.

Native name: Republik Singapura
   (Malay)
German: Singapur
French: Singapour
Spanish: Singapur

ASIA

Sri Lanka

Native name: Sri Lanka (Singhalese)
German: Sri Lanka
French: Sri Lanka
Spanish: Sri Lanka

Democratic Socialist Republic of Sri Lanka

Capital: Colombo
Area: 65,610 sq. km.
Population: 19,232,000
Languages: Singhalese,
Tamil

Currency: Sri Lanka
Rupee
Member: UN
Economy: consumer
goods, machines

The golden lion is the historical symbol of the state, and its sword expresses authority and power. The leaves in the corners of the red ground recall Buddha. The green stripe represents the Muslims, the orange stripe the Hinduistic Tamils. The yellow edge of the flag honors Buddhism, under the protection of which Sri Lanka stands.

Syria

Native name: Suriyah
German: Syrien
French: Syrie
Spanish: Siria

Arabic Republic of Syria

Capital: Damascus
Area: 185,180 sq. km.
Population: 17,384,000
Language: Arabic
Currency: Syrian Pound

Member: UN
Economy: Fuels, foods,
live animals.

The Syrian flag consists of the pan-Arabic colors of red, white, black and green. Red also stands for revolution, white for a glowing future, black for the sorrows of the past. The two green stars recall the alliance between Syria and Egypt, which lasted only briefly. Sometimes the second star is now attributed to Iraq. The flag has exists since 1980.

Taiwan

Republic of China or
Taiwan

Capital: Taipei
Area: 36,306 sq. km.
Population: 22,605,000
Language: Chinese .

Currency: New Taiwan
Dollar
Economy: Electronics,
metals, textiles, plastics,
machines and clocks are
exported

The People's Republic of China regards the island as belonging to China. Taiwan itself already proclaimed the Republic of Taiwan in 1912. In 1971 the UN rejected the Republic in favor of the People's Republic. Taiwan maintains diplomatic relations with 25 countries. The Taiwanese flag consists of a red ground that expresses sacrifice and brotherhood. The blue union stands for freedom and justice, the white sun represents progress.

Native name: T'ai-wan
German: Taiwan
French: Taiwan
Spanish: Taiwán

Tajikistan

Republic of Tajikistan

Capital: Dushanbe
Area: 143,100 sq. km.
Population: 6,305,000
Language: Tajiki
Currency: Somoni

Member: GUS, OSZE, UN
Economy: aluminum,
cotton, metal products

Tajikistan was a republic of the USSR as of 1953 and had a red flag with two thin white red and green stripes. Today red represents the state, white the cotton production and green the agriculture. The crown with seven stars symbolizes the independence of the country.

Native name: Todjikiston
German: Tadschikistan
French: Tadjikistan
Spanish: Tayikistán

ASIA
Thailand

Kingdom of Thailand

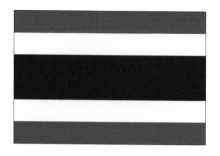

Native name: Prathet Thai, Muang
Thai
German: Thailand
French: Thaïlande
Spanish: Tailandia

Capital: Bangkok
Area: 513,115 sq. km.
Population: 62,014,000
Language: Thai
Currency: Baht

Member: ASEAN, UN
Economy: Machines,
vehicles, raw materials,
foods

In the mid-19th century the flag, then red, was adorned with a white elephant; since 1917 it has borne red, white and blue stripes. Red symbolizes the blood that the Thais would shed for their country, white stands for the purity of the Buddhistic state religion, and blue is the color of the royal house.

Timor-Leste

Democratic Republic of Timor-Leste, or East Timor

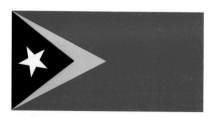

Native name: Timór Loro Sa'e (Tetum)
or Timor-Leste (Portuguese)
German: Timor-Leste
French: Timor Oriental
Spanish: Timor Oriental

Capital: Dili
Area: 14,604 sq. km.
Population: 877,000
Languages: Tetum, Por-
tuguese

Currency: US Dollar
Member: UN
Economy: Coffee is the
chief exportHauptexport-
gut.

In 1975 Timor-Leste, often also called East Timor, declared its independence from Portugal. Since then this flag has existed, to be slightly changed in 2002. Its symbolism is defined in the country's constitution. Red stands for the wealth, black for the bad past before independence, yellow for the fight for independence and white for peace. The star symbolizes the light that leads into the future.

Turkey

Republic of Turkey

Capital: Ankara
Area: 779,452 sq. km.
Population: 70,712,000
Language: Turkish
Currency: New Turkish Lira

Member: NATO, OECD, OSZE, UN, WEU (associate)
Economy: Textiles, clothing, vehicles, iron, vegetables and fruits

Red is the color of the Osmanli or Ottoman Empire, and in 1571 a Turkish fleet used a red flag with three crescent moons in the battle of Lepanto. The crescent moon and star are traditional symbols of Islam, and the crescent moon is associated with Osman, the founder of the empire, and stands for happiness and health.

Native name: Türkiye
German: Türkei
French: Turquie
Spanish: Turquía

Turkmenistan

Turkmenistan

Capital: Ashgabat
Area: 488,100 sq. km.
Population: 4,864,000
Language: Turkmenish
Currency: Manat

Member: GUS, OSZE, UN
Economy: mineral fuels are 86% of the exports.

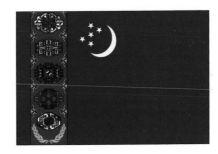

Green is the color of Islam and the traditional color of the Turkic Tatars. The crescent moon also symbolizes Islam, as well as faith in the future. The stars and the five carpet patterns at the hoist symbolize the five regions of the country. White stands for goodness.

Native name: Turkmenistan
German: Turkmenistan
French: Turkménistan
Spanish: Turkmenistán

ASIA
Uzbekistan

Republic of Uzbekistan

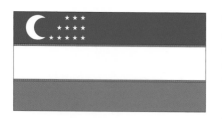

Capital: Tashkent
Area: 447,400 sq. km.
Population: 25,590,000
Language: Uzbekish
Currency: Uzbeki Sum

Member: GUS, OSZE, UN
Economy: cotton fibers, energy carriers, iron and other metals

Native name: Ozbekiston
German: Usbekistan
French: Ouzbékistan
Spanish: Uzbekistán

The blue stripe symbolizes water and sky, the red-bordered white stripe represents peace and purity, and red lines stand for Islam and nature. The new moon stands for Islam, but also for the existence of a new state; the stars stand for the months of the year.

United Arab Emirates

United Arab Emirates

Capital: Abu Dhabi
Area: 77,700 sq. km.
Population: 4,041,000
Language: Arabic
Currency: Dirham

Member: OPEC, UN
Economy: Petroleum, natural gas

Native name: Al Imarat al Arabiyah al Muttahida
German: Vereinigte Arabische Emirate
French: Émirats arabes unis
Spanish: Emiratos Árabes Unidos

All the sheikdoms of which the United Arab Emirates was formed in 1971 had red and white as their traditional flag colors. Green was added when the federation was founded and symbolizes fruitfulness and Islam. Black shows the oil wealth of the land. White also stands at present for the country's neutrality.

Vietnam

Socialist Republic of Vietnam

Capital: Hanoi
Area: 331,114 sq. km.
Population: 81,314,000
Language: Vietnamese
Currency: Dong

Member: ASEAN, UN
Economy: Crude oil, tex-
tiles clothing, shoes

Red stands for the socialistic revolution and the sacrifices that the people had to make for it. The star is a symbol of Communism, and its five points represent the five groups of people in the socialist state: workers, farmers, intellectuals, youth and soldiers. The flag has flown over the reunited land since 1976.

Native name: Viet Nam
German: Vietnam
French: Viêt Nam
Spanish: Vietnam

Yemen

Republic of Yemen

Capital: Sanaa
Area: 536,869 sq. km.
Population: 19,173,000
Language: Arabic
Currency: Yemen-Rial

Member: UN
Economy: Petroleum and
its products

The flag of Yemen consists of the pan-Arabic colors, having the following symbolism here: Red refers to the revolutions that the north and south had to endure to become a united state. The white stripe stands for peace, freedom and prosperity, the goals of the state. Black recalls the hard times of division. The flag was introduced in 1990.

Native name: Al Yaman
German: Jemen
French: Yémen
Spanish: Yemen

GUAM

PALAU

MARSHALL ISLANDS

Majuro

MICRONESIA

NAURU

KIRIBATI

PAPUA NEW GUINEA

Funafuti

SOLOMON ISLANDS

TUVALU

SAMOA

FRENCH
POLYNESIA

FIJI

AUSTRALIA

VANUATU

TONGA

NEW ZEALAND

Oceania is composed of over 7,500 Pacific islands, with an area of 8.5 million square kilometers, and 36.2 million Population. It consists of 14 independent states recognized by the UN: The Australian mainland (plus Tasmania), New Zealand, the Fiji Islands, Kiribati, Marshall Islands, Micronesia, Nauru, Palau, Papua-New guinea, Solomon Islands, Samoa, Tonga, Tuvalu and Vanuatu. There are also numerous islands and island groups that are still overseas territories of France, Great Britain or the USA. The largest country is Australia, the smallest is Nauru. The largest city is Sydney, with 4.15 million Population. Agriculture produces 20% of Australia's economy, with exports including coal, iron ore, gold, sugar, fish, fruit, vegetables and spices.

As varied as the individual states are, so are their Population in origins and ethnic groups. The greater part of the population is of European origin, and there are also Aborigines, Tasmanians, Papuans and Melanesian peoples living on the many islands. The first English settlement was made in 1788, and the British influence is seen clearly in the flags of Australia and New Zealand, as well as Fiji and Tuvalu, which include the Union Jack.

AUSTRALIA/
OCEANIA

Australia

Native name: Australia
German: Australien
French: Australie
Spanish: Australia

Australia

Capital: Canberra
Area: 7,692,030 sq. km.
Population: 19,880,000
Language: English
Currency: Australian
Dollar

Member: OECD, UN
Economy: Ores, metals,
coal, fuels

The Australian flag bears the Union Jack in its upper left corner, a clear indication of the historic connections with Great Britain. The seven-pointed white star represents the six states and the Northern Territory; the five smaller stars are arranged in the form of the Southern Cross, a widespread symbol in the Southern Hemisphere.

Fiji

Native name: Fiji (English)
German: Fidschi
French: Iles Fidji
Spanish: Fiyi

Republic of Fiji Islands

Capital: Suva
Area: 18,376 sq. km.
Population: 835,000
Languages: Fijian, English
Currency: Fiji Dollar

Member: UN
Economy: drinks, foods,
textiles, shoes, tobacco

The blue ground symbolizes the Pacific, the Union Jack refers to the historic connection with Great Britain. The arms show a British lion with four white fields under it, separated by the English cross. The fields show sugar cane, a coconut palm, bananas and a dove of peace.

French Polynesia

French Polynesia

Capital: Papeete
Area: 4,165 sq. km.
Population: 220,000
Languages: French,
Tahitian
Currency: CPF-Franc

Belongs to: France
Economy: coconut oil
and cultured pearls are
exported

French Polynesia is a self-governing overseas
department of France, It consists of five archipelagos: the Society Islands (13 islands), Tuamotu
(76 atolls), the Marquesas Islands (10), the Austral
Islands (5) and the Gambier Islands (14). The best-
known island is Tahiti. The French Tricolor flies
in Polynesia, but the red and white native flag is
recognized. On the white stripe is a double canoe,
with the sun behind it and the sea below. The five
stars stand for the five archipelagos.

Native name: Polynésie Française
(French)
German: Franzo"sisch-Polynesien
Spanish: Polinesia Francesca

Guam

Guam

Capital: Agana
Area: 594 sq. km.
Population: 154,805
Languages: English, Cha-
morro
Currency: US Dollar

Belongs to: USA
Economy: Fish and sweet
potatoes are exported

Guam, the largest Mariana island, is a non-
incorporated territory of the USA and is used
as a naval and air base. Until 1898 Guam was
Spanish; then it was turned over to the USA. The
flag is flown along with that of the USA. The dark
blue stands for the Pacific, the oval in the center
is shaped like a native catapult stone. It shows a
coconut palm that represents perseverance. The
boat is a seaworthy canoe, in which fishermen go
out to sea.

Native name: Guahan (Chamorro)
German: Guam
French: Guam
Spanish: Guam

AUSTRALIA/OCEANIA

Kiribati

Republic of Kiribati

Capital: Bairiki
Area: 810.5 sq. km.
Population: 96,000
Languages: Gilbertese,
English

Currency: Australian
Dollar
Member: UN
Economy: mainly fish
and fish products.

Native name: Kiribati (English)
German: Kiribati
French: Kiribati
Spanish: Kiribati

The blue and white wave lines symbolize the Pacific Ocean. The rising sun stands for a glowing future for the country. The frigate bird is the national bird of Kiribati and symbolizes strength and freedom. The flag is based on the national arms of 1937 and has existed in this form since independence in 1979.

Marshall Islands

Republic of the Marshall Islands

Capital: Dalap-Uliga-
Darrit Area: 181.3 sq.
km.
Population: 53,000
Language: English
Currency: US Dollar

Member: UN
Economy: Fish exported,
mainly to the USA

Native name: Marshall Islands
German: Marshallinseln
French: Iles Marshall
Spanish: Islas Marshall

The blue ground symbolizes the Pacific. The orange stripe stands for prosperity and enthusiasm, the white one for the happy life style of the people. Together they also portray the equator. The 24-pointed star stands for the 24 communities; the longer horizontal and vertical rays form a cross that stands for the people's Christian faith.

Micronesien

Federated States of Micronesien

Capital: Colonia
Area: 700 sq. km.
Population: 125,000
Language: English
Currency: US Dollar

Member: UN
Economy: Fish are 92%
of the exports

The blue ground color symbolizes the Pacific and is also the blue of the UN flag, under whose administration the islands were for decades. The four stars embody the four island groups: Chuuk, Kosrae, Ponape and Yap. Micronesia attained independence in 1979; the flag has flown since 1978.

Native name: Federated States of
    Micronesia
German: Mikronesien
French: Micronésie
Spanish: Micronesia

Nauru

Republic of Nauru

Capital: Yaren
Area: 21.3 sq. km.
Population: 13,000
Languages: Nauruese,
Currency: Australian
Dollar

Member: UN
Economy: 27 million dollar imports against only 9 million exports

The flag reflects the land's situation: The white star stands for Nauru, just south of the Equator (yellow line) surrounded by the Pacific (blue ground). The star has twelve points, one for each tribe of the people. From 1947 to 1968 the island was administered by Australia, Great Britain and New Zealand; then it became independent.

Native name: Naoero (Nauruese)
German: Nauru
French: Nauru
Spanish: Nauru

New Zealand

New Zealand

Native name: New Zealand (English)
German: Neuseeland
French: Nouvelle-Zélande
Spanish: Nueva Zelanda

Capital: Wellington
Area: 270,534 sq. km.
Population: 4,009,000
Languages: English, Maori

Currency: New Zealand Dollar
Member: OECD, UN
Economy: Fish, fruit, animal products, wood

The British Union Jack in the upper left corner attests to New Zealand's connection with Great Britain. The four stars (in four different sizes) are positioned like the Southern Cross and symbolize the double island's position in the Pacific. The flag was officially introduced in 1902.

Palau

Republic of Palau

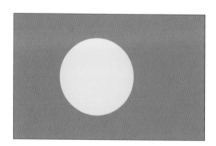

Native name: Belau (Palauish)
German: Palau
French: Belau, Palau
Spanish: Palaos

Capital: Koror
Area: 508 sq. km.
Population: 20,000
Languages: Palauish, English
Currency: US Dollar

Member: UN
Economy: Fish, shellfish and coconuts

Palau became a republic in 1981, and since then the flag with the simple design has flown over the island. Blue naturally symbolizes the sea and sky, while the golden disc shows the moon, which has a very special significance. For the natives, the full moon stands for activities and undertakings, but also for rest, peace and love.

Papua New Guinea

Independent State of Papua-New Guinea

Capital: Port Moresby
Area: 462,840 sq. km.
Population: 5,502,000
Languages: English, Tok
Pisin (Pidgin-English),
Hiri Motu

Currency: Kina
Member: UN
Economy: Gold, copper,
petroleum

Red and black are the dominant colors of art and folklore. The feathers of the bird of paradise also play a major role in ceremonies, and stand for peace and freedom. The stylized Southern Cross indicates the geographical location and the link with other Pacific countries. The flag was introduced in 1971 and retained when independence was attained in 1975.

Native name: Papua New Guinea
(English)
German: Papua-Neuguinea
French: Papouasie-Nouvelle-Guinée
Spanish: Papúa-Nueva Guinea

Solomon Islands

Solomon Islands

Capital: Honiara
Area: 27,556 sq. km.
Population: 457,000
Language: English
Currency: Solomons
Dollar

Member: UN
Economy: Wood, fish,
palm oil

The upper triangle of the flag symbolizes the South Pacific, out of which the Solomons rise—the five stars stand for the five largest island groups. The green triangle stands for the thick vegetation of the islands. The yellow stripe indicates the sun that shines over all the islands. The flag was introduced in 1977; the Solomons became independent in 1987.

Native name: Solomon Islands
German: Salomonen
French: Iles Salomon
Spanish: Islas Salomón

Samoa

Independent State of Samoa

Native name: Samoa (English)
German: Samoa
French: Samoa
Spanish: Samoa

Capital: Apia
Area: 2,831 sq. km.
Population: 178,000
Languages: Samoan, English
Currency: Tala

Member: UN
Economy: Fish products, main buyer is Australia.

The red color stands for courage, blue for freedom, white for purity. The stars in the blue union were borrowed from the flag of New Zealand and represent the Southern Cross, standing for the island state's location in the South Pacific. The present flag was introduced in 1949.

Tonga

Kingdom of Tonga

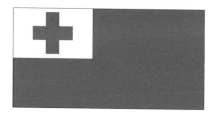

Native name: Tonga
German: Tonga
French: Tonga
Spanish: Tonga

Capital: Nuku'alofa
Area: 748 sq. km.
Population: 102,000
Language: Tongan, English
Currency: Pa'anga

Member: UN
Economy: Foods are the main exports

The cross symbolizes Christianity, the faith of the islanders. The red color stands for the blood that Jesus had to shed to save mankind. The white color symbolizes purity. The king was converted by Christian missionaries in 1862. The flag has existed since 1866.

Tuvalu

Tuvalu

Capital: Funafuti
Area: 26 sq. km.
Population: 11,500
Languages: Tuvaluan,
English
Currency: Australian
Dollar

Member: UN
Economy: Fish is the
main export

Tuvalu became independent of Great Britain in 1978. Since then the flag has existed in the form shown here. The blue ground represents the Pacific, the nine yellow stars indicate the nine islands of the state, which are actually situated in this form. The Union Jack in the union indicates the link with the former colonial power.

Native name: Tuvalu (English)
German: Tuvalu
French: Tuvalu
Spanish: Tuvalu

Vanuatu

Republic of Vanuatu

Capital: Port Vila
Area: 12,190 sq. km.
Population: Bislama,
English, French
Currency: Vatu

Member: UN
Economy: Wood and beef
are exported

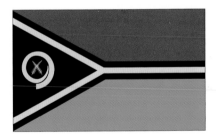

The red part of the flag symbolizes the blood of the people plus the power of their customs. Green stands for the islands and their fruitfulness, black for the population. The yellow Y is a stylized indication of the situation of the islands to each other. Yellow symbolizes peace and the light of Christianity. In the black triangle is the national emblem, a boar's tusk, embodying strength, and two twigs of the namele plant which stands for peace.

Native name: Vanuatu (Bislama)
German: Vanuatu
French: Vanuatu
Spanish: Vanuatu

ARAB LEAGUE

ARAB LEAGUE

Founded: 1945
Purposes: Improving the relations of the member states in terms of politics, culture, society and economy.
Members: 22
Flag: The green color stands for Islam; the white crescent moon in the center is also a symbol of Islam. Over the moon is the name of the league in Arabic lettering, surrounded by a chain that symbolizes unity. A laurel wreath surrounds the chain, standing for peace and security.

EU – European Union

European Union

Founded: 1952-1958
Purposes: Economic cooperation, currency union, common foreign and security policy.
Members: 25
Flag: The blue flag with the circle of stars was introduced in 1955 by the council of Europe. The European Union, which replaced the Council, took over the flag in 1986. Each member state should be represented by a star, but since there are now 25 members, the original form was retained with twelve stars for the 12 founding countries.

ICRC

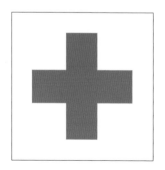

International Committee of the Red Cross

Founded: 1863
Purposes: Promotion of humanitarian rights, protection and help for war victims, supervision of acceptance of the Geneva Convention.
Members: The committee consists of at most 25 Swiss citizens.
Flag: Since the organization was founded in Switzerland, the colors of the Swiss flag were simply reversed to honor that country. In Muslim countries there has been a similar flag, showing a red crescent moon, since 1876 (Red Cross is called Red Crescent there).

NATO – North Atlantic Treaty Organization

North Atlantic Treaty Organization

Founded: 1949
Purposes: NATO was founded in Washington in 1949 by twelve West European and North American states as a security pact. It promotes political, economic and military cooperation to maintain peace and overcome crises.
Members: 26

Flag: The NATO flag was introduced in 1953. The blue ground stands for the Atlantic Ocean, the circle for unity and the points of the compass rose for peace, the main goal of the member countries.

Olympia

Olympia

This flag, known all over the world, was designed by a Frenchman in 1914. The white ground stands for peaceful and brotherly relations of the people with each other and fairness in competition. Each colored ring

stands for a continent: Blue for Europe, black for Africa, red for America, yellow for Asia and green for Australia.

UN – United Nations

United Nations

Founded: 1945
Purposes: Preservation of world peace, respect for human rights, international cooperation for economic, cultural, social, humanitarian and environmental goals. The UN is the world's largest and

most influential organization.
Flag: The UN flag was introduced in 1947. It is light blue and shows a stylized world map, framed by olive branches. Blue and the branches stand for world peace.

Glossary

Banner: A flag hung from a horizontal staff.

Bicolor: A two-colored flag, its field divided equally into two horizontal, vertical or diagonal parts.

Broad Pennant: A flag that tapers to a small end, often used at sea.

Burgee: A small triangular flag, a pennant.

Coat of Arms: The emblem of a family, state or country. Most countries have a coat of arms as well as a national flag.

Dipping a Flag: An international sign of respect of merchant ships for warships; partially lowering the flag one or more times.

Dressed Ship: A ship decorated with signal flags and burgees.

Field: The entire surface of a flag.

Flag: A flag attached firmly to a staff; it is not only a symbol of a country, but may itself be an object of honor.

Flag: A flag hoisted and lowered on a line. A national flag stands for a country.

Flag Mast: A wooden, metal or fiberglass staff on which flags are hoisted.

Flag Raising: The hoisting of a flag in the morning and lowering at sunset, involving expressions of honor.

Floating Cross: A cross whose bars do not extend to the edges.

Flying End: The end of a flag not attached to the mast. In pictures this end is always on the right.

Heraldry: The science of coats of arms.

Hoist: The half of the flag close to the mast or staff.

Merchant Flag: The flag that shows the nationality of merchant and private ships.

Pan-African Colors: Green, yellow and red. They go back to the Ethiopian flag..

Pan-Arabic Colors: Black, white, green and red. They go back to the Jordanian flag.

Pan-Slavic Colors: White, blue and red. They are based on the Russian flag.

St. Andrew's Cross: A diagonal cross usually extending to the edges of the flag.

St. George's Cross: A central cross made of a horizontal and a vertical bar, extending to the edge of the flag.

Scandinavian Cross: A cross displaced in the direction of the hoist.

Service Flag: A special form of a national flag used by agencies of the country, and usually bearing a coat of arms.

Shield: A family, city or national coat of arms in the form of a shield.

Standard: The flag of a head of state.

Stars and Stripes: The flag of the USA.

State Flag: A decorated version of a national flag, used only for service purposes.

Tricolor: The French flag, or any other flag divided horizontally or vertically into three equally large parts.

Union: The upper left corner of a flag. Originally the bow flag of warships in harbors.

Union Jack: The national flag of Great Britain, with the crosses of St. George, St. Andrew and St. Patrick.

Vexillology: The science of flags and flag information.

Index

Index